DROPA
Legends & Lore

Connecting the Ancient Secrets of Bhutan, China, Nepal, Tibet, and Sirius

HANS DIETRICH

ISBN: 979-8-9936378-1-5

Hans Dietrich

4110 SE Hawthorne Blvd. #323,

Portland OR, 97214

www.megamyst.com

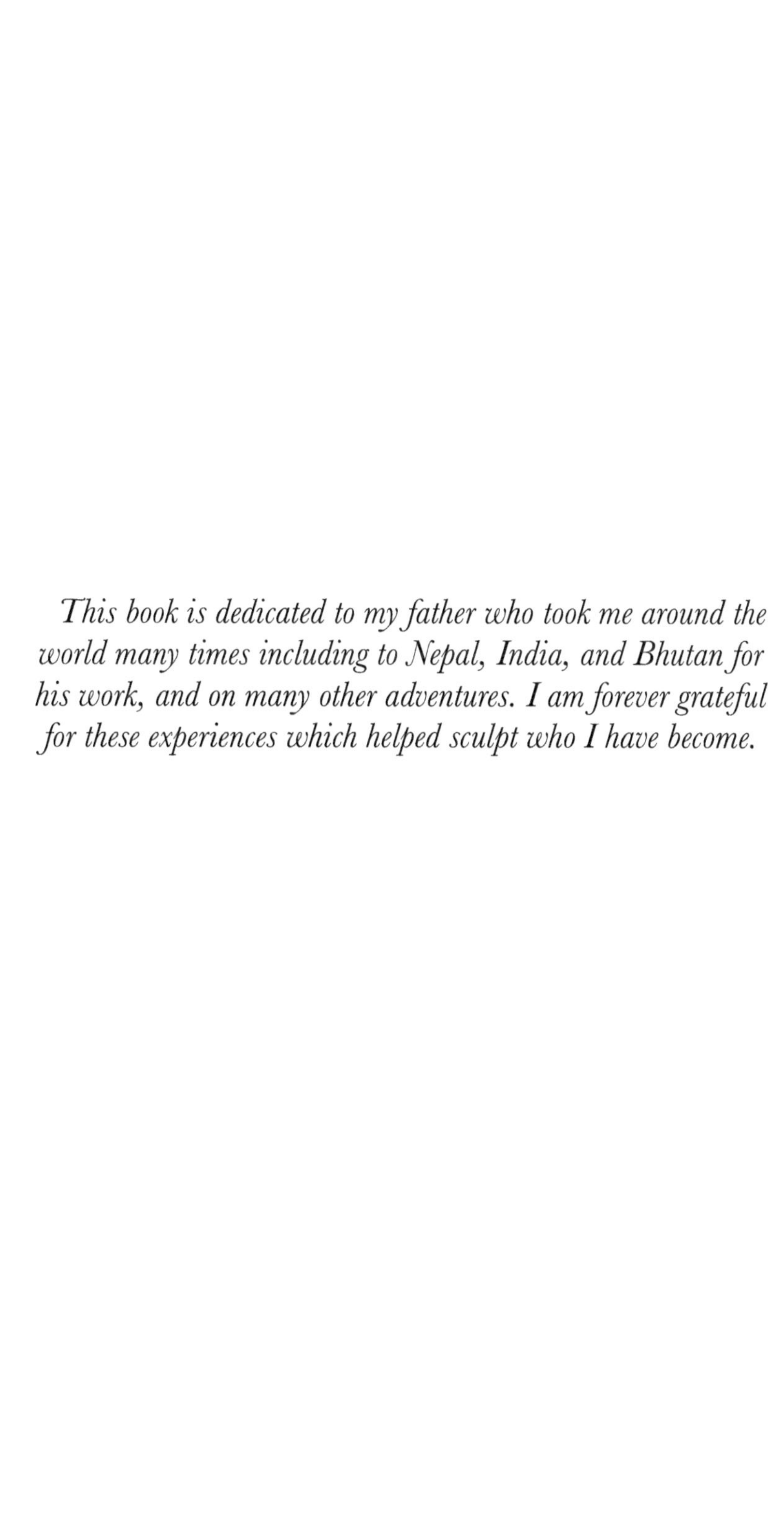

This book is dedicated to my father who took me around the world many times including to Nepal, India, and Bhutan for his work, and on many other adventures. I am forever grateful for these experiences which helped sculpt who I have become.

Table of Contents

A forewarning for the remainder of this book: the content herein reflects my personal research, education, interpretations, and viewpoints on the subjects under discussion.

Interest In the Dropa

Lately, there has been a surge of online documentaries and blog posts centered around the lore and legends of the Dropa Stones and the Dropa people residing in the Bayan Kara Ula Mountain range in far eastern Tibet. After examining numerous articles and mini documentaries addressing this subject matter, I noticed that they all appear to regurgitate the same handpicked details from a 2004 episode of the UFO Files, which Wikipedia also repeats. There is a lack or mention of genuine research into the origin of this tale, or a scholarly approach to the information provided. Most of what I came across briefly discusses the meager information presented in the documentary, which scholars are swift to deem phony or fraudulent. Due to the restricted and incredible nature of the data available on the lore and legend of the Dropa, I embarked on a mission to authenticate and collect as much information as possible before drawing any conclusions about its legitimacy.

As I reflect on my personal journey, which includes growing up in Kathmandu Nepal and traveling extensively throughout South Asia, a memory stands out from 1998 when I encountered a group of nomadic individuals called the Drokpa in Bhutan. I couldn't help but wonder if there was a connection between these people and the ones mentioned in the various online stories and publications regarding the Dropa. Fast forward to the autumn of 2020, when I stumbled upon one of my friend and lecturer Jonny Enoch's posts on the topic and shared my curiosity with him. To my surprise, he challenged me to delve deeper and gather more information about the Dropa Stones.

Initially, my intention was to disprove the legitimacy of the Dropa Stones story and dismiss it as a falsehood or a hoax. As is my usual approach when studying esoteric topics related to ancient civilizations, artifacts, and peoples, I typically start with a high level of skepticism and a long list of questions to answer, with the aim of debunking such claims. However, my interest in the topic, coupled with a possible link through my studies in Bhutan, motivated me to conduct a thorough investigation into the Dropa. I endeavored to gather as much information as possible, examining how it might relate to other historical events, cultural mysticism, and lore from the past. In this way, I approached the topic of the Dropa Stones, and what follows are my personal insights and opinions based on the research I conducted. Through my findings, I discovered a connection between the Dropa and their origin in Sirius, as well as a link to ancient Buddhist cultural mysticism, sutras, and related stories.

First Discovery of The Dropa Story

https://www.youtube.com/watch?v=0KF16vY6WHU

I became familiar with the Dropa story while watching episode 15 of the UFO Files on the History Channel in December 2004, after meeting a tribe of nomadic Tibetans known as the Drokpa in Bhutan six years prior.

The show featured discussions from well-known UFO researchers including Richard Dolan, David Serada, and Hartwig Housdorf, who authored "The Chinese Roswell". They delved into the intriguing tale of the Dropa, as well as related stories such as "Sungods in Exile", which had been featured in publications like Sputnik Magazine, the Belgian UFO Bulletin, and Vegetarian Universe from 1962.

The UFO researchers presented an elaborate narrative around the Dropa Stones, covering various details from their initial discovery in a cave in central China in 1938, to a supposed translation of an alien language two decades later in 1958, to scientific investigations on the disks conducted in the Soviet Union in the late 1960s, and even to the alleged discovery of dwarves in a village named Huilong, which could be any one of over ten Huilong villages in China.

However, despite their claims of the Dropa stories being a hoax without providing any substantial evidence, I found their account lacking in proper research and sought to uncover a more plausible explanation through my own extensive investigation into the topic. I set out as a sceptic myself to discover or disprove as much as I could based on the crumb trail provided by the researchers in this documentary, which has gone on to influence almost all of the other research about Dropa without further investigation by other researchers in this field.

The rest of this book is dedicated to my life's adventures leading up to my thesis studies in Bhutan and my extensive research into the materials relating to both the Dropa story and its connection to Sirius and the Sirius connection to Buddhist cultural mysticism.

My History Growing up in Nepal

In 1981, I relocated to Kathmandu, Nepal, due to my father's job in anthropology and social forestry, although I was born in Washington state. He had already been visiting Nepal since his time with the Peace Corps from 1962 to 1964 as a part of group 2 and had completed his doctoral dissertation in a remote Gurung village in 1970, where he spent a year studying the social or caste-based structure of the village and the interactions among its inhabitants.

Author and sister at her 8th birthday, 1981

Growing up in Nepal, I was just 5 years old when I first experienced the chaos of the monsoon rains, a phenomenon that was entirely new to me. However, I had already witnessed the spectacular eruption of Mount Saint Helens in Washington state the year before, when I was just 4 years old. After celebrating my 5th birthday in mid-September, my family embarked on a trek to the remote village of Sikrung, located high up in the Manang valley in Gorkha district. The village clung precariously to the side of a cliff, and it was where my father had completed his doctoral dissertation, studying the social and caste-based structure of the village over the course of a year.

Interestingly, Sikrung was located very close to the epicenter of the devastating 2015 earthquake in Gorkha district, which prompted me to contact NASA for assistance in obtaining GIS photography of the region. This information was crucial in identifying which roads and bridges were destroyed, and in coordinating the supply convoys that brought much-needed aid to the affected remote villages. I am grateful for NASA's assistance, which proved to be a success in delivering crucial aid to those in need.

Sikrung village, Gorkha, Lumjung Nepal, 1981

At Sikrung, during the Dashain fall festival, my sister (8) and I (5) were the esteemed guests. The festival was held to celebrate a successful fall harvest and the start of spring planting for the next year's harvest. The festival involved the sacrifice of an animal, such as a buffalo, goat, or chicken, depending on the family's status and wealth. The blood of the animal was then spread over all machines and tools used by the villagers, including cars or trucks, bicycles, and plows. The head of the animal was typically chopped off by a shaman, and the meat was distributed equally among the village families, who then prepared a grand feast consisting of flattened rice, vegetable curry, raksi (a moonshine of sorts), warm chang (similar to nigori or cloudy saké), fresh yogurt, Nepali chai, and the entrails of the animal fried up (such as brain, stuffed intestine, heart, stuffed lung).

Village Shaman dancing around buffalo with katana sword, 1981

It was during this festival that I was introduced to the cultural mysticism and magic of village shamanism. The shaman emerged with a white, skeletal face and seduced the buffalo with his movements and sword, which in this case was a Katana or Samurai sword taken from a Japanese officer during WW2 by the headmaster of the village in Brunei during a very bloody ground war. The shaman danced around the buffalo until the animal closed its eyes and lowered its head, hypnotized by the movement. In one swift motion, the shaman sliced off the head of the buffalo. My sister and I were then blessed by the villagers, and we all feasted on the unfamiliar food, which was a new experience for me at the time.

Author being blessed by the late King Birendra, Nepali New Years, 1982

During my time in Nepal, I received the king's blessings on Nepalese New Year and learned about the Mahābhārata from the older sons of our housemaid. The Mahābhārata tells the story of an epic 18-day war between the gods who returned to earth from Mahar in their flying temples and ships, after a great solar outburst that had destroyed life on Earth thousands of years before. The gods discovered that their children and the humans who had populated the planet were still alive, leading to a great war of the land, which is what "Mahābhārata" means. The war is described in a way that resembles science fiction, and it even mentions weapons such as the famous Brahmāstra, which has effects like those of a nuclear bomb.

Artistic depiction of the Mahābhārata

I also gained knowledge of a being called Kutch-kundi, a succubus who appears as a distressed woman dressed in white. She can often be found at night on trails or roadsides, begging for assistance. It is worth noting that white garments are typically associated with the death of a parent, often the father, and Kutch-kundi is therefore seen as a symbol of mourning. She is said to have feet that face backwards and a string trailing behind her. Once she ensnares an unsuspecting man, she walks backwards along the string until she reaches a hole in the ground where she then hypnotizes and devours her victim. Another similar creature is the Baan Juga, also known as the forest leech, a small humanoid that resides in the jungle and preys on people or animals that stray from the path or become lost.

Thirdly, I discovered the legend of the Yeti, also known as the local Big Foot, who purportedly inhabits high Himalayan caves. While sightings are rare, their howls can be heard at night, and they occasionally attack stray villagers and livestock, although they generally keep to themselves. The Pangboche monastery, located between Tengboche monastery and Everest Base Camp, houses a famous Yeti scalp and hand, and numerous footprints have been found in remote regions of the Khumbu area, in both snow and dirt. They are said to emit a putrid garlic odor and are spotted throughout Nepal, Northern India, Bhutan, and even Central China.

My initial encounter with the Yeti was through a graphic novel titled "Tintin in Tibet," by Belgian artist Herge, which is highly recommended for those unfamiliar with Herge's comics from that era. A summary of the book follows.

The storyline of "Tintin in Tibet" follows a passenger plane en route to Europe that crashes into the Himalayan region. Sadly, Tintin's young Chinese companion, Chang, was aboard the

Tintin in Tibet, Herge, 1958

plane, but fortunately, he is rescued by the elusive Yeti. In the end, Tintin manages to rescue his friend from the Yeti's cave, high up in the Himalayas. Throughout the book, readers are taken on a journey exploring the magical and mystical aspects of Tibet, with Tintin and Captain Haddock meeting lamas and monks who possess the ability to levitate themselves and religious instruments through deep meditation. This is reminiscent of the tale of Drakpa Gyeltsen, the ascended Tulku lama, which is also discussed in this book under the "Ascended masters of Sirius" section. "Tintin in Tibet" also introduces the legendary creature known as the Yeti, Himalayan Big Foot, or Abominable Snowman, which was relatively unknown to Western audiences around the book's publication in 1958.

Growing up in Nepal during the early 1980s without access to computers or television, I relied on the stories from my childhood

Author reading Star Wars, 1982, and character Chewbacca from Star Wars

and the occasional movie screening at the international club in Kathmandu for entertainment. These tales, along with my vivid imagination, inspired me to create my own adventures, which often featured Star Wars-inspired space and yeti encounters. I used various household items, such as masking tape, cardboard boxes, toothpicks, wine corks, and dried coconut shells, to bring my imaginative worlds to life. Interestingly, Chewbacca, a beloved character from the Star Wars saga, served as my inspiration for the Yeti figure in my stories, as his physical appearance closely resembled that of the legendary creature.

Despite experiencing the revolution in Nepal in 1990, where I was shot at and tear gassed, which is a story for another time, I am proud to have graduated from Lincoln School in Kathmandu with several notable achievements. I was honored to serve as the Student Council Treasurer, a member of the National Honor Society (NHS), and the captain of our International School Basketball team, which placed second and first in the SAISA (South Asian School Association) Championships several times. Additionally, I excelled in my AP math and science classes, placing among the top students in my class. Lincoln School is a smaller South Asian International School with a student body of 320 from kindergarten through 12th grade, including about 68 students in high school and representing 72 nationalities. As a result, I developed a close-knit community of friends from various age groups and cultural backgrounds.

Internship in Nepal

Depiction of Kathmandu, Nepal 1998

After attending Pacific NW College of Art (PNCA) in Portland, Oregon, I pursued a proposed contract major that combined traditional graphic design and illustration with the emerging field of web and interactive design. Upon completing my third year of studies in 1998, I returned to Nepal and worked as an intern for SignMakers (p)ltd., a start-up large format print company. My six-month job was to train the staff on the newly purchased machines from Singapore, create designs for local brands such as Tuborg, Carlsberg, Kukri Rum, Shikar, Surya, Kathmandu International Airport, Pokhara Airport, Dusit Thani Fulbari Resort Hotel, Soaltee Royal Holiday Inn, Casino Anna, and Casino Nepal, to name a few. I also found ways to streamline the design and printing process. I successfully accomplished my final task of training the manager and his staff, and these experiences proved valuable later when I designed large format textile prints for fashion design purposes.

Intensive Thesis Study in Bhutan

Tiger's Nest Monastery, Bhutan, prior to burning down, 1998

During the summer of 1998, I embarked on an intensive two-month thesis study in Bhutan to explore its cultural mysticism, art, and architecture. Bhutan is a nation that still reflects the lifestyle of a 15th century nation, making it a unique and challenging destination to travel to. Fortunately, I was granted an invitation to visit, as Bhutan is notoriously difficult to obtain a visa for. The Swiss, Nepalese, and Indians are permitted entry as they share borders and have helped develop local industries such as poultry farms, creameries, and distilleries. However, other Westerners must obtain an invitation and pay a $200-300/day visa fee, with a minimum stay of 10 days and a cap of around 2,000 tourists per year, at that time. Visitors are also limited to certain areas, typically sites around the capital of Paro and a 9+ hour drive to Bumthang, with restricted access to more remote Dzongs and Lhakhangs. Thankfully, I was granted special permission to visit these areas and conduct my thesis research, as my father worked in Bhutan at the Institute of Forestry in Trashigang in the far east of Bhutan.

Author studying at the and Jakar Dzong, and Kharchu Dratshang Dzong, Bumthang Bhutan, 1998

The First of Three Rooms

Thangka painting of Ugyen Wangchuck, 1998

I had a translator who accompanied me to various Dzongs and Lhakhangs that were rarely, if ever, visited by westerners. During my visit to the Kharchu Dratshang monastery in Bumthang, I saw a large thangka painting depicting a procession for the first Dropa, Drukpa, or Druk Gyalpo (Cloud Dragon King) of Bhutan, Ugyen Wangchuck or Deb Nag-po, his Drukpa name. The procession featured pilgrims from all over, including a British traveler who brought ivory tusks from an elephant hunt as a gift, and a Drokpa nomad carrying the Cintamani stone from its dimensional resting place of Shambala. This thangka was considered auspicious as it had been struck by lightning several years earlier, which descended through the thangka and the dharmachakra or bhavachakra mandala in the center depicting the cycle of life. According to legend, the Drokpa founded Bhutan and they practice Nyingma Pa Buddhism, which is one of the oldest lineages of Buddhism and is known for its magic, sorcery, and ascended tulku masters.

Drokpa nomadic with Singing Bowl and Cintamani Stone, 1998

For reference, the Cintamani stone is a significant symbol in Buddhism and is believed to have descended from the dimensional mountain of Mount Meru to Earth via a rainbow bridge from Sirius. Along with the stone, three other items were said to have come in the box. The Vajra Dorje, a lightning bolt symbolizing Vajrayana Buddhism; The Buddha's Bowl, a singing bowl depicting resonance and vibration; and the Ohm Mani Stone, a circular stone with engravings of the enlightenment mantra "Ohm Mani Padme Whom". For more information, refer to "The Four Gifts from Sirius".

Druk cloud dragon on the Bhutanese flag

Interesting facts to note are that the national flag of Bhutan depicts the Druk or Cloud Dragon, while the term "Nag" in Sanskrit and Shina refers to the Great Serpent, which is often depicted as a deity or human with a snake or dragon's lower body and a human's upper torso. Additionally, the language of Shina, which predates the regional mother language of Sanskrit by several thousand years, is spoken by nomadic tribes in the region extending from the Black Sea to central Tibet, and other versions of this language spoken in the area include Brokskat and Brokkat, primarily spoken by the Drokpa people.

Depiction of a Naga Deity

Naga or Snake Deities in Popular Movies

It's worth mentioning that throughout this book, I will draw on ancient concepts that are also depicted in contemporary movies. For instance, one such concept is that of the Naga, which can be seen in several modern Western films. Three examples that stand out are:

Thulsa Doom, the leader of an ancient and magical snake cult in "Conan the Barbarian" (1982). He transforms himself into a snake during the course of the film, but is ultimately defeated by Conan, which breaks the spell of the cult and frees its folowers.

Thulsa Doom, Conan the Barbarian, 1982

An additional illustration is found in the movie "The Golden Child" (1986), where Kala, the Dragon Lady, an ancient goddess rescued from Tibet, foretells the future to the protagonist, Chandler Jarrell, from behind a curtain. Jarrel in disbelief tears down the curtain to reveal the true nature of Kala and her half human, half snake or Naga body.

Kala, the Dragon lady, The Golden Child, 1986

An example from more recent times is the character Medusa in the movie "Clash of the Titans" (2010). In the movie, she is defeated by Perseus, who is the son of Zeus and a human, while her head and stare that turns men and beasts to stone, is used to defeat the Kraken sea monster.

Medusa, Clash of the Titans, 2010

The Second of Three Rooms

The room of the Meditator, Bhutan, 1998

In another room of the Lhakhang, there was a fascinating depiction of "the meditator," portrayed as a long-haired sage performing various life duties on the walls. The entire room was covered with artistic depictions of the meditator and became a long part of my studies.

The character is shown in different forms, resembling the Hindu deity Shiva, Siddhartha, or Shakyamuni, and even Milarepa, meditating for the world. The meditator is also illustrated as a hunter, a farmer, a fisherman, a lover, a father, and more. It was here that I learned about the Boddhisatva of the Buddha Siddhartha, or Shakyamuni as he is known in the East.

This term Boddhisatva refers to a human who has the ability to reach enlightenment or Nirvana in one lifetime, but instead of ascending to the astral realms, chooses out of compassion, to remain behind and assist others in overcoming suffering within their lives. Both Siddhartha and Milarepa are depicted as devout Bodhisattvas in this room.

The Third of Three Rooms

Depictions of Mount Meru. Ascended Masters, Demons and Fertility, Bhutan 1998

A third room that was shown to me was strictly off-limits to women, although women are not typically permitted in the monasteries. The room was painted entirely in black, with yellow and white outlined art covering the walls. The paintings depicted scenes of demons devouring humans, as well as the angry spitting penis that is a common motif in Bhutanese art, painted on house walls to promote fertility. Additionally, the paintings included the image of the penis catcher, a woven pouch that is traditionally hung outside of houses for the same fertility purposes.

Fertility art on traditional Bhutanese house, 1998

In addition, there were also illustrations resembling the Kamasutra, portraying the union of gods, humans, and demons. Furthermore, there were depictions of the four precious gifts that descended from Sirius, according to legend, and became the foundational pillars of Buddhism.

It is said that these gifts, which include the Cintamani stone, the Vajra Dorje, the Singing Bowl, and the Mani Stone, were brought to the earthy realm 20,000 years ago and placed in a sacred box which was stored in the sacred and mystical city of Shambala for safe keeping.

The Four Gifts from Sirius

According to legend, the Ascended masters from Sirius sent four gifts, that were placed in a sacred box. These gifts descended from the dimensional realms of Mount Meru and appeared to the Great Buddha around 20,000 years ago, predating the time of Siddhartha, who is often regarded as the first Buddha but was only a reincarnation of the Buddha. The four gifts are:

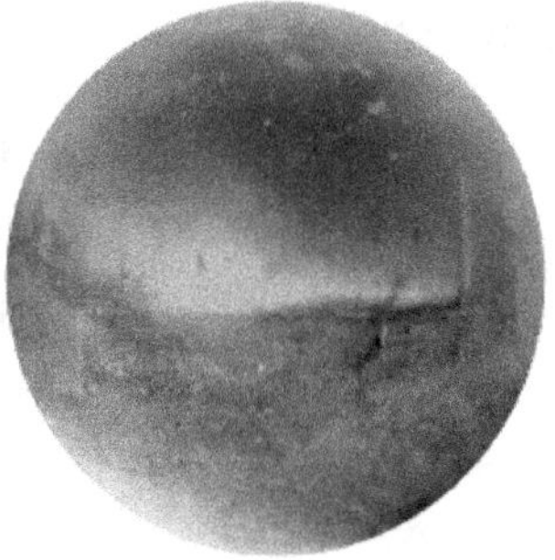

The Cintamani Stone, a moldavite glass or piece of a meteor, also known as the wish fulfilling gem, luck stone, or even the dream stone. It is said that the Cintamani stone grants its possessor longevity of life and good fortune.

The Vajra Dorje a gold, 4-sided lightning bolt, represents the four cardinal directions and fuor elements that are the symbol of Vajrayana Buddhism, is said to grant the followers of this sect enlightenment within one lifetime, becoming a Boddhisattva, allowing them through the meditational spiritual technology of astral projection, to return to its source, of Sirius.

The Singing Bowl or buddhas bowl, representing harmonic frequency, oscillation, and meditative entrainment of the mind.

The Ohm Mani Stone is a circular stone with the Tibetan mantra "Ohm mani padme hum" engraved on it. Reciting this mantra during meditation can grant clarity and perfection on the path to enlightenment. The mantra translates to "the jewel within the lotus," where the jewel symbolizes boundless compassion that responds to suffering and moves us to alleviate it unconditionally and spontaneously. The lotus represents the pure heart of awakening that is rooted in the mud below the water's surface. While the lotus is the crown chakra, the jewel also represents the seat of consciousness, the pineal gland, and both the lotus flower and the pineal can produce trace amounts of DMT, which could help in establishing an enlightened state of mind.

According to legend, when the four items gifted from the Ascended masters from Sirius arrived on Earth, the Cintamani Stone was separated from the box and concealed in the mystical underground city of Shambhala by the great Buddha, who was also known as the King of the World. Despite this, it is said that shards of the stone managed to find their way back to our world and have since been sought after for thousands of years.

Davinci's Salvatore Mundi, 1499-1510, and the Kaaba Stone in Mecca

The Cintamani stone has been the focus of empires and secret societies for thousands of years, and it has been depicted and described in various ways. Leonardo da Vinci famously included it in his painting Salvatore Mundi, a painting depicting Jesus Christ holding a perfect crystal sphere, representing the Holy Grail or Philosopher's Stone of immortality, while to Muslims, it is housed within a silver yoni and known as the Kaaba stone, sitting in the eastern corner of the black cube building in Mecca, Saudi Arabia. It is believed to be a meteor that fell from Sirius, the brightest star in the east, during the hajj that takes place around mid-June to early July when Sirius is first seen on the horizon in the northern hemisphere. The stone has also been depicted as a perfect crystal sphere, given as a gift to the Great Buddha or other Buddhist leaders, as seen in Thangka paintings of Bhutan's first king, Ugyen Wangchuck. Additionally, it is considered a lucky stone and is placed under the paws of the Fu Dogs guarding the entrance to the Forbidden City in China.

The Great Buddha and the Fu Dogs of China

The final representation of the Cintamani stone is intriguing, as the luck stone guarded by the Fu Dogs which stand guard to the Forbidden City in China and is adorned with the flower of life symbol. Sirius is commonly associated with the dog star, making the Fu Dogs an interesting topic. In Tibetan culture, Sirius is referred to as the Sirius Earth Dog and is particularly visible in the sky every 60 years. The most recent occurrence was in 2018, with the previous one being in 1958. This date is noteworthy and may be linked to the connection between Sirius and the Dropa story, which emerged in the late 1950s and early 1960s.

Tiangou, the Heavenly Dog and Zhang Xian

The Chinese have named Sirius as Tiangou, which translates to *Heavenly Dog*, a mythical creature resembling a black dog star or meteor. It is believed that during an eclipse, Tiangou devours the sun or the moon. Chinese mythological character Zhang Xian is often depicted shooting at Tiangou to safeguard his children who are clustered around him. This symbolizes the protection of the people of the land from cataclysm.

During World War I, pilots engaged in aerial combat, which were called dog fights. In World War II, pilots reported being chased by glowing green orbs, which they nicknamed Fu or Foo Fighters. It's interesting to consider whether there could be a connection between these descriptions and the dog star Sirius and the Cintamani stone.

Foo fighters from WW2

In addition, the Cintamani stone has made its way into Hollywood as esoteric symbolism in the movie Wonder Woman 1984. In the film, the stone is referred to as the Dream Stone, a Greek and Buddhist symbol that grants whoever possesses it the gift of luck, wishes, and dreams.

When the main antagonist, Max Lord, gains possession of the stone and then crushes the stone to absorb its power, in Buddhism he would be known as Cintamani Loksavara, the embodiment of the Cintamani stone and its powers.

Max Lord and the Dream Stone, Wonder Woman 1984

Cintamani Loksavara

The Legends of Mount Meru

Mount Sumeru, also known as Mount Meru, is a fascinating subject. It is described as both a physical mountain in Tibet and a place of great worship and reverence. However, it is also depicted as a stacking of dimensions that ascend from the inner earth where Shambala and Shangri-la are said to be located, through the dark and gritty dimensions inhabited by beings, to the earthly plains and their inhabitants, and into the heavenly realms and their inhabitants. At the top of the mountain is the stupa, where a rainbow bridge is described and depicted as ascending into the void of space and time towards Sirius in ancient times. The bridge could be a depiction of the milky way ascending into the sky from the horizon or the mountain, however, today, Buddhism teaches that the bridge ascends to the pole star or Polaris. It is unclear when this change occurred as there are references to both stars being the destination point the mountain points towards.

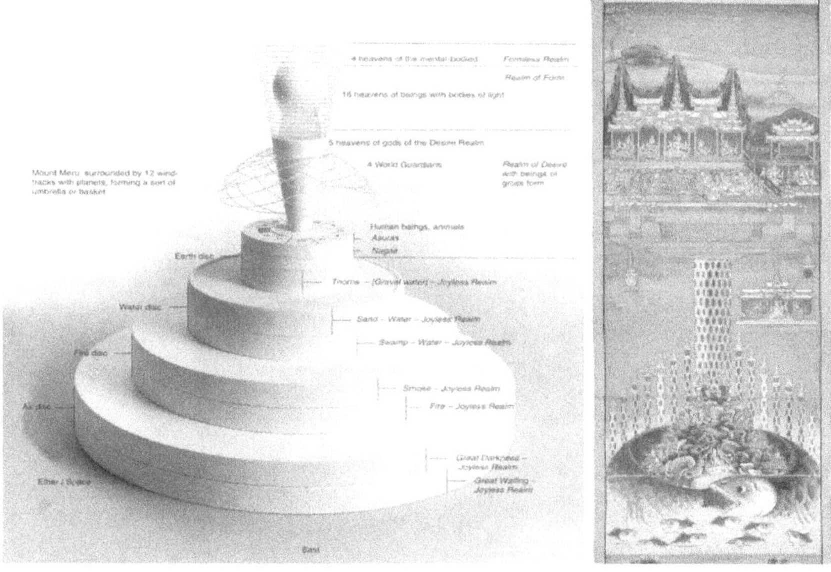

Depictions of Mount Meru and the rainbow bridge to Sirius

It is worth noting that Michael Cremo, a Vedic creationist, and alternative archaeologist, presents a similar description of Vimanas.

Michael Cremo, https://www.youtube.com/watch?v=d8VNTZOc9aY&t=56s

According to Cremo, some Vimanas are made of solid metal and are inhabited by flesh-and-blood beings, while others are aetheric and occupied by light beings, among other types. It is said that demons have also ascended and descended the mountain to prey upon the Earth and humans. However, the mountain is most renowned for the four gifts from Sirius and the journeys of a few ascended or tulku masters.

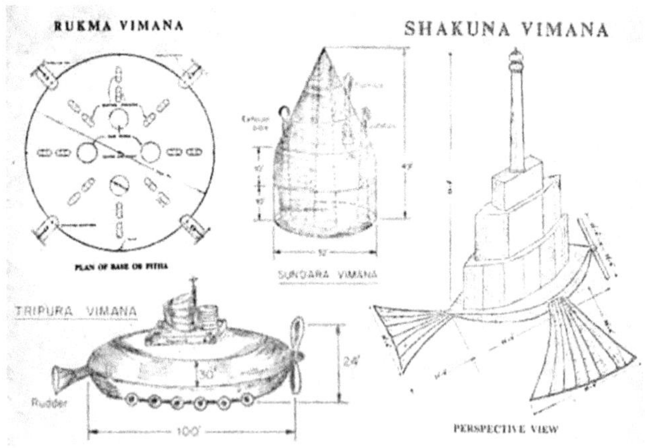

Depiction of types of Vimanas from Vaimānika Shāstra, 1918

Ascended Masters and the Life of Siddhartha

Depiction of Gautama Siddhartha aka. Gautama Śākyamuni

When I was in high school in Nepal, I first encountered the story of the Ascended Master, Siddhartha, which is well-known among scholars and Buddhist practitioners worldwide. The story is told in Herman Hesse's book "Siddhartha", first published in German in 1922. Christopher C. Gregory-Guider wrote an excellent summary and detailed analysis of the book for Britannica.com in 2017.

The novel's central theme is the search for self-realization by Siddhartha, a young Brahman who abandons his comfortable life to wander in search of serenity and to experience the contrasts of life with equanimity, including joy and sorrow, life, and death. He tries asceticism, wealth, sensuality, and the attentions of a lovely courtesan but finds no satisfaction. Finally, he goes to the river and learns to listen, discovering within himself a spirit of love and accepting human separateness. In the end, Siddhartha achieves a state of bliss and highest wisdom.

As the son of a Brahmin, Siddhartha enjoys a life of privilege in his home village, but his heart is moved by a burning desire to acquire wisdom and new experiences. He and his childhood friend, Govinda, leave home to join the Samanas, a group of wandering ascetics. As the novel unfolds, we follow Siddhartha in his search for meaning and truth in a world of sorrow and suffering, drawing on both Hindu and Buddhist teachings. Hesse challenges our ideas of what it means to lead a spiritual life, emphasizing the importance of seizing the reality of each moment rather than blindly adhering to any system of belief.

The novel's potent symbol of a river conveys the sense of vibrancy and flux in life, and the prose flows as naturally and shimmeringly as the surface of the river beside which Siddhartha spends the final years of his life.

What the novel doesn't mention are the many relations that Gautama Siddhartha Śākyamuni has with the stars of Sirius. As previously mentioned, two of his deciples, Ascended Tulku Master is Mahā-maudgalyāyana and Bodhisattva Manjushri both have had encounters with Sirius. Mahā-maudgalyāyanaastral projected himself from the top of Mount Meru acros the rainbow bridge of time and space to Sirius where he encounterd a race of giants, while Manjushri had an astral and physical encounter with Ascended Tulku Master Gadgadsvara, an extraterrestrial from Sirius who came to Earth atop his flying palace, a tower of sevel levels, crossing the dimensions of time and space accompanied by the sounds of hundreds of thousands of musical instruments.

Ascended Masters and the Life of Milarepa

Depiction of Ascended Master, Milarepa

Ascended Master, Milarepa (1052-1135), was born in the Gungthang province of Western Tibet near Nepal and experienced a difficult childhood and youth. At the age of seven, his father passed away, and his relatives mistreated his family by taking over their property. Milarepa's embittered mother sent him to learn black magic to seek revenge against those who had wronged them. Milarepa became skilled in the practices he was taught and caused destruction by killing many people.

After realizing the negative impact of his actions, Milarepa sought to shed the bad karma he had accumulated during his vengeful youth. He sought guidance from Nyingmapa Lama Rongton, who recognized Milarepa's karmic connection to Marpa and sent him to study with him. Marpa exposed Milarepa to a rigorous apprenticeship, including building and tearing down rock towers to Marpa's specifications with his bare hands, to purify himself from the negative karma he had acquired. After years of hard work and perseverance, Marpa transmitted all the Mahamudra teachings from Naropa, Maitripa, and other Indian masters to Milarepa.

Milarepa secluded himself in isolated mountain retreats and practiced these teachings for many years until he attained enlightenment. He became well-known for his perseverance in practice and spontaneous songs of realization, and Gampopa became his primary lineage holder among his many students.

The Ascended Masters of Sirius

In Buddhism, there exist many Ascended Tulku Masters, who are lamas or monks that possess the ability to master spiritual meditation technology of astral projection, and ascend or descend into the dimensional realms of time and space, as depicted in the Mount Meru experience.

Spiritual technology differs from mechanized technology as it pertains to repeated cultural or religious practices meant to alter the mind, body, and spirit of the practitioner. Throughout this book, I will use the term spiritual technology, and it is best to describe its meaning here. Meditation, like fire, is one of humanity's earliest spiritual technologies.

Out of the numerous Ascended Masters, I found myself most intrigued by those associated with Sirius. Although I learned about Siddhartha, who became the Buddha after discovering his compassion for human suffering and becoming a Boddhisattva to assist humanity, and Milarepa, a Siddha who found enlightenment and forgiveness after being accused of murder by becoming a devoted Buddhist and Boddhisattva, I was most captivated by the teachings of three specific Ascended Tulku masters. Two of these masters originated from Earth and travelled beyond time and dimension to the stars, including Sirius, while the third was believed to have originated from Sirius, the brightest star that rises in the east and is revered in Buddhist philosophy, culture, and even its origin through the four gifts, considered foundational pillars.

What is an Ascended Tulku Master?

An Ascended Tulku Master is a fusion of an individual who has attained the highest level of spiritual evolution, becoming a light body through meditation, and an enlightened being of love and light. In Buddhism, a tulku is the physical manifestation of an enlightened Buddhist master, achieved through extensive meditation, which can ultimately result in the ability to levitate and even consciously travel the dimensional cosmos using meditational spiritual technology such as a Merkabah or an astral projected form.

The Merkabah, which translates to "light-spirit-body," is an energetic sphere or sacred octahedron that encompasses all existence. It serves as a vehicle for traveling to all dimensions, including those of unity and love that transcend the mind. The Merkabah consists of interlocking tetrahedrons facing upward and downward, symbolizing the duality of existence between body and spirit, unified in a singular and harmonious form. The octahedron fills the inner void and resonates with our emotional body, creating a singular light.

It's worth noting that ancient knowledge such as Merkabah use and astral projection is also depicted in modern movies, although the origins of such concepts are often overlooked as viewers become absorbed in the story and visuals.

The Fountain, 2006

For instance, the movie "The Fountain" (2006) features the protagonist Tommy, who is tasked with bringing the sacred seed information of the Earth tree or fountain of youth back to its source in Xibalba, the Mayan underworld or place of fright. However, in the movie's story, Xibalba is depicted as a stellar nursery near the belt of Orion and serves as a place of rebirth. Tommy travels through the cosmos in a sphere resembling a Merkabah, with the milk of the tree and sacred waters, guided by his emotions and love, to reach this place of rebirth and start anew. The movie is a moving tale that spans historical events, the past where Tommy is portrayed as a conquistador challenged by the Queen of Spain to find the fountain of youth and tree of life in South America. To the present where Tommy's wife is dying of cancer, while writing the book about the conquistador. And to a future world and time, also depicted in a novel she has written that he must finish. Overall, it's an epic, exciting, and emotional movie that's definitely worth watching.

The Empire Strikes Back, 1980

The movie "The Empire Strikes Back" (1980) features a scene where Darth Vader is shown in his Merkabah chamber, which he uses to heal his burnt body and explore his emotions. This chamber also allows Vader to project his consciousness to his son Luke, the Emperor, and other Jedi and Sith practitioners, showcasing its ability to expand spiritual consciousness. Additionally, the Star Wars Saga introduces us to the concept of the Enlightened Tulku Light Body through Jedi Master Obi Wan Kenobi, who appears in this form to Yoda and Luke on Dagobah in "The Empire Strikes Back". This concept is also depicted in "Return of the Jedi" (1983), "Star Wars: The Last Jedi" (2017), and "Star Wars: The Rise of Skywalker" (2019).

Star Wars: Return of the Jedi, 1983

Star Wars: The Rise of Skywalker, 2019

In "Star Wars: The Last Jedi", we witness Luke utilizing astral projection to confront his nephew Kylo Ren on the salt planet of Krate, projecting his physical form from Ach-to. This ability is further shown in "Star Wars: The Rise of Skywalker", as Luke appears to Rey after she discards his lightsaber into the fire from Kylo's burning TIE Silencer, which she had taken from him on Endor in her search for the Sith way finder. Master Yoda is also portrayed as a golden light body in "Return of the Jedi", "The Last Jedi" and "The Rise of Skywalker", highlighting that this concept and skill is acquired through intensive Jedi and Sith training.

Star Wars: The Last Jedi, 2017

Another interesting symbology shown here is that while Luke is astral projecting himself, he is able to levitate, and while he is dying from the strength it takes him to complete this, feat he is staring into the setting sun. In ancient Khemit (ancient name for Egypt) this would have been called "westing" or dying into the sunset to be reborn again.

One of the most captivating illustrations of astral projection in cinema comes from Disney/Marvel's 2017 film, "Dr. Strange". In the movie, the Ancient One, the Sorcerer Supreme, expels Dr. Stephen Strange's astral form from his body and reveals to him the vastness of space and time. These are all examples of occult symbolism presented in Hollywood for entertainment purposes but hold a much deeper significance to those initiated in such philosophies.

Dr. Strange, 2017

This is where we delve into the three ascended and tulku masters I learned about while in Bhutan and have since researched further, starting with Drakpa Gyeltzen.

Ascended Master Drakpa Gyeltzen

Thangka of Tulku Drakpa Gyeltsen

Drakpa Gyeltsen, a Tulku who lived from 1619 to 1656, is known for his ability to levitate himself and his ritual instruments and objects during intense meditation. He was also know to be able to have total recall of past events and prophetic visions during meditation and prayer. His name is derived from "Drukpa," which means "of the cloud dragon". Having mastered the meditational spiritual technology of physical and astral projection, he is often depicted in thangka paintings traveling from Mount Meru to Sirius in his astral or Merkabah energy form, using a rainbow bridge.

At the Tamshing Lhakhang in Bumthang Bhutan, where he is venerated, monks enter the Holy of Holies, a pitch-black room used for intensive sensory deprivation meditation. To stay grounded, they wear a heavy chainmail during meditation, that is often staked into the ground, preventing their body and soul from being lifted from the earth into the dimensions of Mount Meru and being lost in time and space. The name Drakpa is related to Druk, Drokpa, and Dropa through transliteration.

Thangka of Tulku Drakpa Gyeltsen and the rainbow bridge to Sirius
Monk with heavy chainmail used for intense meditation

The concept of astral projection or traveling from one point in spacetime to another through a supposed wormhole, also known as an Einstein-Rosen bridge, is a hypothetical structure based on a special solution of the Einstein field equations.

A noteworthy point is that the concept of the Einstein-Rosen bridge is also mentioned in the movie "The Last Mimzy" (2007). In the movie, the character Noah Wilder discovers how to create three-dimensional mandalas for time travel, which is also known as a "rainbow bridge" based on Einstein and Rosen's mathematical theories on time and dimensional travel.

The Last Mimzy, 2007

Additionally, in the Disney/Marvel movies featuring Thor, the character Heimdall can transport Thor and other Asgardian heroes using a similar technology called the Bifrost, which is visually represented as a rainbow bridge and the entrance to Asgard.

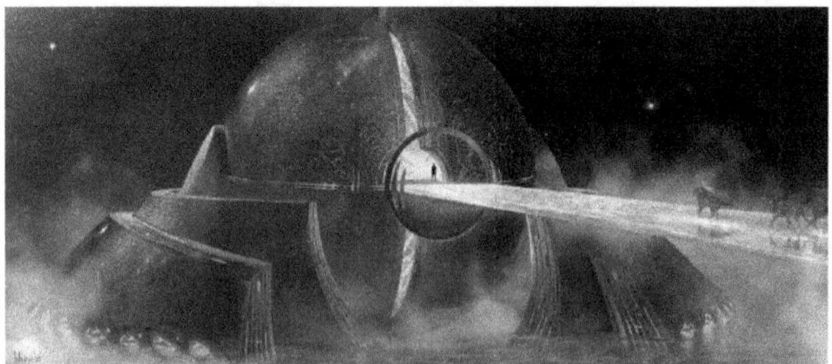

Rainbow bridge of Asgard

Ascended Master Mahā-maudgalyāyana

Ascended Tulku Master Mahā-maudgalyāyana

The second Ascended Tulku Master is Mahā-maudgalyāyana, an enlightened disciple of the historical Buddha Śākyamuni who lived around 600 BC. According to legend, he used his Merkabah meditation spiritual technology to travel to the distant Sirius solar system. He climbed the dimensions of Mount Meru to the summit to hear the loving voice of the Buddha, and upon realizing that he could, he asked Śākyamuni to grant him the ascension technology of the great masters so he could travel the galaxy to the brightest star to the east of Earth, Sirius, to hear the Buddha's voice again. He was granted the techniques to travel in Merkabah form, and he arrived at a planet in the Sirius system inhabited by giant people who mistook him for a bug. However, the Buddha of that world recognized him as a bodhisattva of Śākyamuni and welcomed him to practice under his guidance, making him an ascended master of Sirius. Mahā-maudgalyāyana is also said to have possessed the ability to shape-shift, see ghosts or apparitions, and even fly.

Ascended Master Gadgadasvara

Ascended Master Gadgadasvara accompanied by musical instruments

The third Ascended Tulku Master is mentioned in chapter 23 of the *Lotus Sutra*, written around 100 BC, and is known as Gadgadasvara, an extraterrestrial Bodhisattva from Sirius. Through deep meditation and guidance, he was able to astral project himself in a psychic form on Earth in front of Buddha Śākyamuni and his disciple Bodhisattva Manjushri after sending a message of seven-jeweled lotus flowers. Manjushri asked the Buddha about Gadgadasvara, and the Buddha explained that he was a sage, a Bodhisattva from another world that exists around the brightest star that rises in the East, Sirius.

Manjushri then requested to learn the space-travel Merkabah meditation technique and if Gadgadasvara could visit them in flesh. Śākyamuni informed Manjushri that because he was not initiated in the meditational spiritual technology of astral projection, he would have to be guided. Manjushri then was guided into deep meditation and met with Gadgadasvara on the astral plane and invited him to visit earth in his physical form. Gadgadasvara accepted the challenge and climbed atop his flying palace, a tower of seven levels, and with the sounds of hundreds of thousands of musical instruments he crossed the dimensions of space and time from Sirius to Earth. Gadgadasvara appeared in his physical form at Earth, descended the tower, with golden sparkling skin, short stature, and deep blue lotus-like eyes. Interestingly, the description of his light body is like that of the Dropa people with yellow-gold skin and blue eyes.

Gadgadasvara then blessed Śākyamuni, Manjushri, and the deciples of the Buddha and said the Earth was a beautiful place unlike the Saha, or mundane world that he had come from, destroyed by war and filled with muck, filth, rocks and mountains. Mounting the tower again he departed, accompanied by the sounds of hundreds of thousands of musical instruments, and returned to his own world around Sirius, crossing the dimensions of time and space. The Buddha explained that Gadgadasvara had the ability to shape-shift and take on different human, dimensional and anthropomorphic appearances if desired.

The depiction of the flying palace and tower and the cacophony of musical instruments could possibly be a representation of incomprehensible technology at the time, perhaps a starship and the sounds of its engines. It's also interesting to consider whether his astral projection was a type of holographic technology, like what we see in the Star Wars movies.

Solo: A Star Wars Story, Dryden Vos' Yacht Tower, 2018

The 2018 movie "Solo: A Star Wars Story" features a tall tower descending from the clouds, namely Dryden Vos' Yacht Tower Ship, which may be of similar depiction, including the sounds of it's repulsor engines. Additionally, holographic technology is frequently depicted throughout the Star Wars film franchise, first introduced in Star Wars Episode IV, A New Hope, 1977, when the robot R2D2 projects Princess Leia's message for Obi-Wan Kenobi.

Star Wars Episode IV, A New Hope, 1977

The Drokpa of Bhutan, Nomads from Far East Tibet

Depiction of the Drokpa nomadic people of Bhutan

During my research, I came across the Drokpa, a group of nomadic people in Bhutan who originated from far East Tibet. While the Drokpa have been nomadic for some time and have migrated through various regions such as Central China, Far East Kham Tibet, Tibet, Bhutan, Northern India, Nepal, Ladakh, Kashmir, Afghanistan, Turkmenistan, and into the Black Sea region, it was during the Chinese invasion of Tibet in 1950 that most of them were forced into a permanent nomadic lifestyle. This invasion resulted in the loss of their homeland and the eradication of many of their people under the Maoist regime.

As the Drokpa migrated through different regions, their name changed through transliteration, starting with the Dropa in eastern Tibet, to Dzopa in central Tibet, to Drokpa in Bhutan and Nepal, and then Brokpa in northern India and Ladakh, and as they traveled further west.

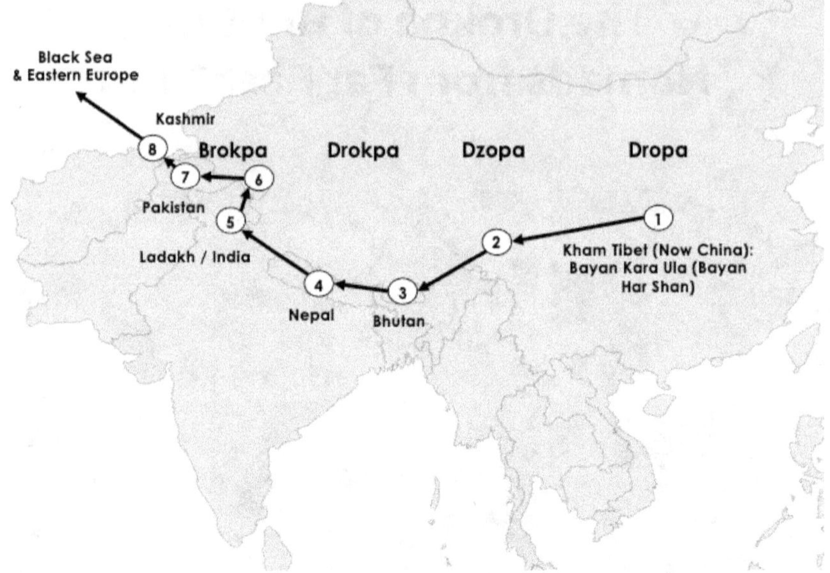

Map showing Drokpa nomadic path from far east Tibet

The Drokpa people are easily identifiable by their short stature and unique clothing, which includes a leather vest with wool lining and a spider cap made of felted wool to protect them from the rain and cold weather. Due to their language barrier, they remain mysterious and enigmatic to outsiders. However, they have had a significant impact on the development of Bhutan and the Nyingma Pa sect of red hat Buddhism.

The Drokpa were instrumental in translating Buddhist scriptures from Sanskrit into Tibetan and Hindi, which contain accounts of magic, sorcery, and the incredible abilities of Ascended Tulku Bodhisattva Lamas, such as the meditational spiritual technology of astral projection, levitation, and even shapeshifting in human, dimensional, and anthropomorphic forms.

It is worth noting that in this photo, the Drokpa woman is standing next to my seated mother, who is only 5 foot 4, indicating that the Drokpa woman is likely no taller than 4 feet.

The Drokpa and Brokpa communities speak a form of Shina language that predates other languages in the region, including ancient Chinese, Tibetan, Nepali, Hindi, and even the mother language, in the region, of Sanskrit. There are a few variations of Shina, such as the endangered Brokkat language spoken by descendants of Drokpa yak herd communities in Bhutan's Bumthang Valley, and the Brokskat or Minaroskat, an Indo-Aryan language spoken in Ladakh and Gilgit-Baltistan regions of Pakistan and Kashmir.

Shina language, spoken by the Drokpa/Brokpa people and other tribes in Northern Pakistan, Afghanistan, and Kashmir, dates to between 4000-5000BC, making it much older than Sanskrit. It is a gendered language like Spanish or Thai, with both a male and female tongue, and a caste or class-based language with a common tongue and an upper-class or royal tongue.

Interestingly, the Dropa in the story"Sungods in Exile" (1978), speak a dialect very similar to Shina, which is also a gendered and caste-based language. This leads us to the main question and focus of this book: who exactly are the Dropa?

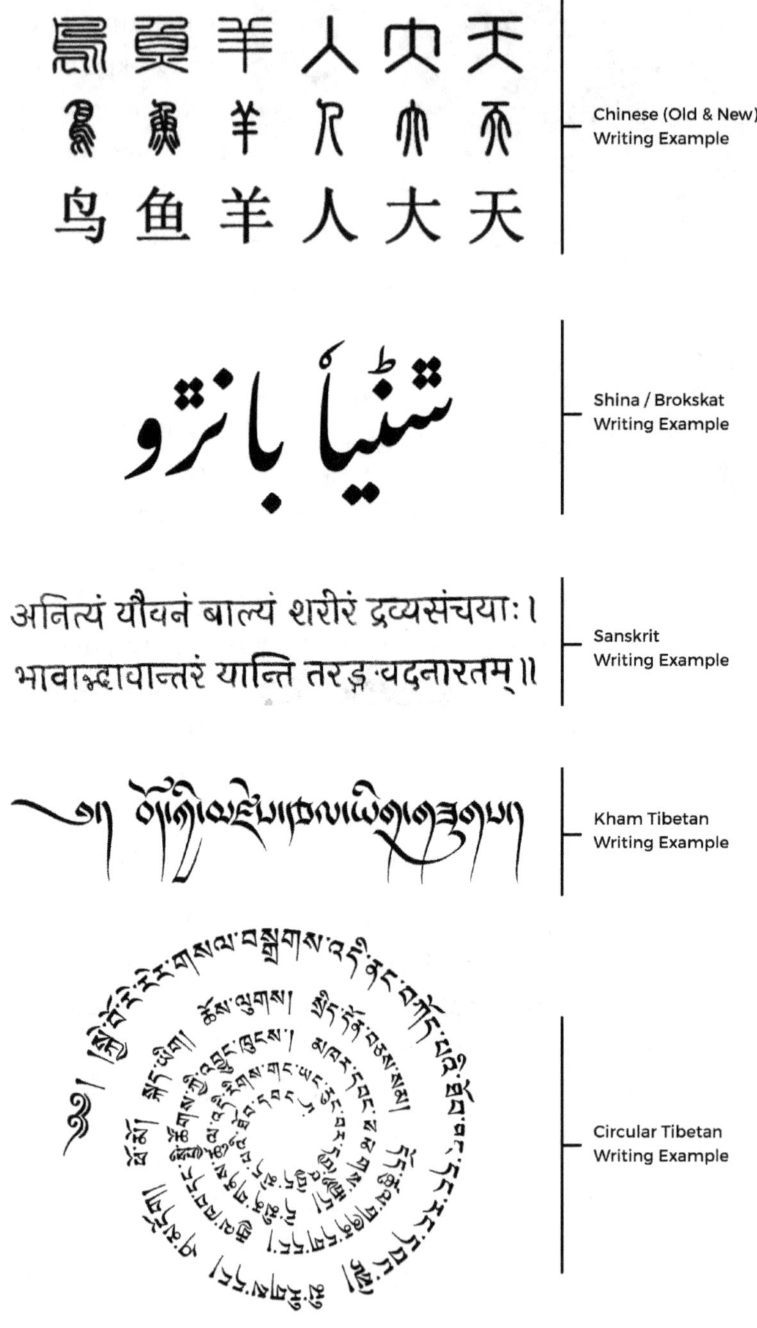

Examples of Chinese, Shina / Brokskat, Sanskrit, Kham Tibetan, and Circular Tibetan writing

The Dropa Stones, Lore and Legends

https://www.youtube.com/watch?v=0KF16vY6WHU

At the outset of the book, it is mentioned that the author's first encounter with the lore and legend of the Dropa was through the 2004 History Channel documentary on the Dropa and the Chinese Roswell. The documentary features UFO researchers Richard Dolan, David Sereda, and author Hartwig Hausdorf, who was interviewed for the program. In the documentary, the story is told of an archeologist named Chi Pu Tei and his team who, in 1938, journeyed to the remote regions of China and Eastern Tibet, where they discovered a cave in the Bayan Kara Ula Mountain range. Inside the cave, they found petroglyphs on a flat wall that was hewn from the bedrock using an unknown cutting technique. The petroglyphs purportedly depicted the rising sun, the moon, a star system (which the researchers suggest may be our own solar system but is also thought to be Sirius and Canis Major), and a dotted line leading to a mountain range, presumably the Bayan

Kara Ula and Bayan Har Shan range on Earth. In the back of the cave, they discovered neatly arranged skeletons or mummified remains of short-statured people with large, "clumsy" heads, as Hausdorf describes them, yellowed orange skin, and blue eyes.

Along with the bodies, a disk about one foot in diameter was discovered, featuring a central hole and two lines spiraling from the center to the outer edge, with micro-hieroglyphs in an unknown, foreign, and potentially alien language that could only be studied through a magnifying glass.

Depiction of Chi Pu Tei, aka. Shifu Tei and the Bayan Kara Ula expedition, 1938

After the initial discovery of the first disc, the team proceeds to excavate the cave and find 716 more discs. Years later, in 1958, a deciphering attempt is made by Professor Tsum Um Nui from the Beijing Academy of Prehistory (also known as the Beijing Academy of Sciences by the researchers). The researchers consider the translation impossible as Nui has no cipher to crack the code. However, to their surprise, the disks reveal that the Dropa crash-landed in the Bayan Kara Ula mountains around 12,000 years ago, which is contrary to what the researchers initially believed.

Upon conducting further research, I found that the 2004 UFO Files History Channel Documentary on the Dropa and Chinese Roswell, which introduced me to the lore and legends of the

Dropa, lacked depth in their understanding of the story of the "Sungods in Exile."

The researchers' knowledge of the story seems to have come from the blurb on the back cover of the book, rather than the actual content. Had they delved deeper into the content with an understanding of Buddhist cultural mysticism and cultural phenomenon, they would not have dismissed it so easily as a hoax. The researchers claimed that elements of the story and characters within it could not exist, but their conclusion was based on inadequate research, in my opinion. They cited a 1998 publication of Fortean Times in which the author of the book admitted hoaxing the book, but I purchased and have read the book several times and arrived at the opposite conclusion.

While the documentary is entertaining and raises many interesting questions, I wondered if the researchers conducted any research into the origins of the Dropa story. Typically, these documentaries have a pre-written script that the actors and researchers follow, giving their opinions on the topic. However, this approach does not lend itself to integrity-based research.

According to the UFO researchers, the Dropa story originated in a German publication called "Vegetarian Universe" in 1962, "The Belgian UFO Bulletin" from the same year and even popular Soviet publication, "Sputnik Magazine". However, my research has not yielded any evidence of this story or these publication's existences in 1962 Germany, Belgium or even the Soviet Union. Despite my best efforts, I could not find any articles, editions, or publications of Vegetarian Universe or the Belgian UFO Bulletin that suggest that they ever existed.

However, the short-lived nature of the German UFO publication UFO Nachrichten suggests that Vegetarian Universe may also have been short-lived. This makes it difficult to follow the trail and raises the possibility that later researchers may have been misdirected.

UFO Nachrichten, the 1964 German UFO Bulletin

According to my research on the Dropa story, the earliest publication I could find was a translation of a 1964 German UFO News or Bulletin article, which briefly mentioned a Vegetarian Universe article from two years prior. The researchers in the UFO Files documentary also referred to the "Belgian UFO Bulletin," but I could not locate any evidence of its existence as stated. It is possible that this refers to the German newspaper UFO Nachrichten, published by the Deutsche UFO-Studiengemeinschaft (DUIST) from 1964 to 1966. As Belgium and Germany share the Germanic language, this could explain why the "Belgian UFO Bulletin" is so difficult to find and may be another attempt at poor research or misdirection to support the hoax narrative.

One of the most significant misinterpretations of the original source stories stems from the translations or transliterations. In the original German, the story refers to the Dropa and Kham tribes in far eastern Kham Tibet, now central China where the Bayan Kara Ula mountains are located. However, in the later Sputnik translation, the name for the Kham tribes was changed to the Ham tribes, which have no historical record as a cultural group in China. While there is a Han dynasty in Chinese history, the Ham tribe simply does not exist in my research. This raises the question of whether this is another attempt at misdirection or simply a transliteration error. Based on my research, it appears that the supposed Ham tribe is actually the Kham Tibetans of this region in far East Tibet.

According to the translation from the 1964 "UFO Bulletin" from German to English, Tsum Un Nui translated the groove writings and stated that they tell of aerial vehicles from a time long ago, around 12,000 BC. However, the disk translation itself does not mention a specific date. It appears that the date is significant and connects to another story and timeline, which we will discuss later. In the meantime, here is what was translated from the disks:

"The Dropa came down with their air gliders from the clouds, ten times until the sun set. The men, women and children hid in the caves, and saw that the Dropa came this time in peaceful intention."

Ufos in der Vorzeit?

Die Hieroglyphen von Baian-Kara-Ula

Archäologe Tsum Um-nui: „Rillenschrift kündet von Luftfahrzeugen vor 12 000 Jahren"

Wir werten es als gutes Zeichen, daß auch Zeitschriften anderer Fachgebiete wie z. B. „Das Vegetar. Universum" nachstehenden Artikel seinen Lesern zur Kenntnis brachte. D. Red.

(DINA), Tokio

Im Grenzgebiet zwischen Tibet und China liegt das Höhlengebiet des Baian-Kara-Ula-Hochgebirges. Hier sind schon vor 25 Jahren die merkwürdigen Schrifttafel- und Hieroglyphenfunde gemacht worden. Mit unauffindbaren und völlig unbekannten Geräten sägten vor mehreren tausend Jahren Menschen, von deren Aussehen die chinesischen Forscher nur vage Vorstellungen haben, aus härtestem Granitgestein schallplattenförmige Teller. Die bisher in den Höhlen des Baian-Kara-Ula aufgefundenen 716 Gesteinsteller weisen auch genau wie Schallplatten in der Mitte ein Loch auf. Von dort bewegt sich eine Doppelrille in Spiralenform zum Außenrand. Dabei handelt es sich natürlich nicht um Tonrillen, sondern um die eigenartigste Schrift, die jemals in China und wohl auf der ganzen Welt gefunden wurde.

Es dauerte über zwei Jahrzehnte bis Archäologen und Wissenschaftler alter Schriften und Hieroglyphen die Schriftrillen entziffern konnten. Der Inhalt ist so verblüffend, daß die Akademie für Vorgeschichte in Peking den Bericht des Gelehrten Prof. Tsum Umnui anfangs gar nicht veröffentlichen wollte. Dann tat sie es doch. Mit vier Kollegen kam Archäologe Tsum Um-nui überein: „Die Rillenschrift kündet von Luftfahrzeugen, die es den Schriftplatten nach vor 12 000 Jahren gegeben haben muß." Wörtlich heißt es an einer Stelle: „Die Dropa kamen mit ihren Luftgleitern aus den Wolken herab. Zehnmal bis zum Aufgang der Sonne versteckten sich die Männer, Frauen und Kinder der Kham in den Höhlen. Dann verstanden sie die Zeichen und sahen, daß die Dropa diesmal in friedlicher Absicht kamen. . ."

Funde der Dropa- und Kham-Rasse sind in den Höhlen des Hochgebirges schon früher gemacht worden. Archäologen können diese nur bis zu 1,30 Meter großen, also sehr kleinen Menschen heute noch nicht völkerkundlich unterbringen. Es besteht keine Parallele zu den Chinesen, Mongolen oder Tibetanern. Man kann natürlich vermuten, daß sich schon vor Jahrtausenden ein Schriftkundiger der Kham einen Scherz erlaubt hat oder daß es Aberglaube war, als er von „Luftfahrzeugen" berichtete. Was sollte dann aber die Aussage anderer Rillenhieroglyphen der Kham bedeuten, die, will man jede Sensation ausklammern, schlicht einen Klagegesang darüber darstellen, daß die eigene „Luftflotte" bei der Landung in dem schwer zugänglichen Gebirge zerstört wurde und es keine Mittel und Wege gab, eine neue zu bauen.

Die Hieroglyphen von Baian-Kara-Ula scheinen der chinesischen Archäologie so mysteriös, daß sie nur mit Vorsicht wissenschaftlich davon Gebrauch macht. Man hat Gesteinspartikel von den Schrifttellern geschabt und zur Analyse mit einer Kohlenstoffuhr nach Moskau geschickt. Dabei wurde eine sensationelle Entdeckung gemacht: Die Rillenplatten sind stark kobalt- und metallhaltig. Beim Test einer ganzen Platte mit einem Oszillographen zeigte sich ein überraschender Schwingungsrhythmus, so, als wären die Platten mit der Rillenschrift einst „geladen" gewesen oder hätten irgendwie als elektrische Leiter gedient.

Niemand kann sagen, was hinter diesen Rillenschriftplatten aus der Zeit vor 12 000 Jahren steckt. Mutmaßungen wären zu gewagt und nicht objektiv genug. Man erinnert sich aber der alten chinesischen Sage von den kleinen dünnen, gelben Menschen, die „aus den Wolken" kamen und wegen ihrer Häßlichkeit — ungewöhnlich große und breite Köpfe auf spindeldürrem Körper — von allen gemieden und von den „Männern mit den schnellen Pferden" (Mongolen?) getötet wurden. Tatsächlich fanden sich in den Höhlen Grab- und Skelettüberreste aus der Zeit vor 12 000 Jahren. Tatsächlich wiesen die als Dropa- und Kham-Rasse bezeichneten Funde Maße eines schmächtigen Körperbaus und gewaltigen Schädels auf. In ersten chinesischen Archäologie-Gutachten ist von einer „ausgestorbenen Gebirgsaffenart" die Rede. Aber hat je jemand von geordneten „Affengräbern" gehört und „Schriftplatten", die Vorzeitaffen angefertigt hätten?! Im Jahre 1940 ist der Archäologe Tschi Pu-tei für diese Theorie in ganz Asien verhöhnt worden. Tschi Pu-tei verteidigte sich aber, indem er erklärte, die Skelettfunde seien seiner Überzeugung nach Affen gewesen, die Rillenschriftplatten wären von späteren „Kulturen" in den Höhlen abgelegt worden.

Das alles ist etwas wirr. Aber es ändert nichts an dem Hieroglyphen-Rätsel von Baian-Kara-Ula, das dadurch nur noch komplizierter wird, daß die Höhlenwände Ritzbilder der Schriftplatten aufweisen, mehrfach die aufgehende Sonne zeigen, den Mond und die Sterne und dazwischen, ganze Schwärme erbsengroßer Punkte, die sich in elegantem Schwung dem Gebirge und der Erdoberfläche nähern.

Reinhardt Wegemann

Sputnik Magazine from 1967

The documentary also refers to an article in the Soviet/ Russian "Sputnik Magazine" from 1962. However, this article first appeared in Sputnik Magazine from 1967 under the title "Cosmic Visitors" by UFO and anomalies researcher Vyatcheslav Zaizev, a similar researcher to that of Linda Moulton Howe.

I came across a French version of the article and had it translated, which recounted the original story from the 1964 German UFO Bulletin, including the strange and possibly false Vegetarian Universe reference. Although some of the names and translations differ slightly, this is in my opinion likely due to transliteration anomalies.

The article describes the same origin story of Chi Pu Tei's archeological expedition, the dating of the materials, and the miraculous translation of the disks, which are not from the Dropa's perspective. The Sputnik article also expands on the scientific tests carried out on at least one of the disks, although we do not know how they gained access to the disc(s). The scientists discovered that the jadeite disks contained cobalt and mercury after analyzing small fragments of the stone material, and they conducted oscillation tests that revealed an unusual rhythm of vibrations, leading to the conclusion that the disks had been charged or had been part of an electrical circuit. Unfortunately, we do not know what happened to the disks after these tests, and the article moves on to other historical UFO topics.

What Happened 12,000 Years Ago

The date of 12,000 years ago holds significant importance in the history of our planet. According to researchers Graham Hancock and Randall Carlson, this date marks the end of the ice age and the beginning of the Younger Dryas period, which was a smaller secondary ice age that we are still emerging from today. This period was sparked by the Holocene comet impact event, which is believed to have caused Meltwater Pulse 1B, a catastrophic flood that rapidly melted ice sheets and flooded the planet, leading to widespread destruction of both flora and fauna and almost wiping out humanity.

For Hancock, this period is also significant because it is when Plato placed the fall of Atlantis, a worldwide and advanced civilization, despite mainstream history suggesting that the world was only populated by hunters and gatherers at that time. The discovery of ancient ruins like Göbekli Tepe in Turkey, Gunung Padang in Indonesia, and the ancient city of Dwarka off the coast of India, which were all above water 12,000 years ago, challenges our current understanding of history.

In the Edfu Egypt hieroglyphics and a depiction found at Karnak in Egypt, a mass exodus from an ancient landmass and cataclysm is described, which is believed to be the fall of Atlantis. In summary, the history of Atlantis is a period of time rather than a specific place and holds great significance in our understanding of ancient civilizations and cataclysmic events that may have shaped our planet's history.

Plato's Atlantis is a story that appears in two of Plato's dialogues, Timaeus and Critias. In these dialogues, the character of Critias tells the story of Atlantis as it was told to him by his grandfather, who heard it from the Athenian statesman Solon, while he was in Egypt.

Edfu Egypt temple texts & glyphs depicting the exodus from Atlantis, 12,000 years ago

According to the story, Atlantis was a powerful and advanced civilization that existed over 9,000 years before Plato's time (12,000 years ago roughly). The Atlanteans were said to have conquered many parts of the Mediterranean world and even parts of Europe and Africa.

The civilization was described as having a highly organized society and a sophisticated culture. However, over time the Atlanteans became corrupt and began to exhibit hubris, which ultimately led to their downfall.

The gods punished the Atlanteans by causing the island of Atlantis to sink into the sea, leaving behind only a few remnants of their once-great civilization. Even the clairvoyants Edgar Cayce and Rudolf Steiner discuss in detail their channeling of Atlantis and its downfall, after a harnessing of technology that brought about their destruction.

The story of Atlantis has captured the imagination of people for centuries, and many have searched for evidence of its existence, including Howard Hughes, Hemmingway, Jacques Cousteau, Stephen Hawking, and Mercury Astronaut Gordon Cooper, to name a few. Much of Atlantis is thought a myth, however Cayce discussed Atlantis rising in the precise area that the Bimini Road was discovered under the ocean off Bimini, and off the shore of Cuba, Pauline Zalitzki, a marine engineer discovered sunken ruins of a complex city.

The relevance of the 12,000-year date in the Dropa Stones' original translations lies in the fact that the Dropa supposedly arrived in Tibet at this time in their winged gliders. The reason for their arrival is still a mystery, as they may have come from an extraterrestrial planet around Sirius, traveled through the dimensions of Mount Meru and a rainbow bridge from Sirius, or escaped the cataclysm and great flood during the fall of Atlantis, the Holocene comet impact event, Meltwater Pulse 1B, and thus the beginning of the Younger Dryas.

Interestingly, one of the legends of Atlantis is that many of its inhabitants originated from Sirius, making it intriguing that all three stories share Sirius as an origin point for the Dropa. Although the Dropa story does not overlap with the timeline of Atlantis, it is fascinating that their arrival coincides with the events of Atlantis's fall. Additionally, the concept of Shambala is also worth exploring, and we will delve into this concept further in this book.

Sungods in Exile, a Possible Hoax?

David Agamon's book "Sungods in Exile" (1978) recounts scientist Karyl Robin-Evans' 1947 expedition to the Bayan Har Shan and Bayan Kara Ula region where he encountered the Dropa, an indigenous tribe of only a few hundred people. According to the book, the Dropa revealed that their ancestors arrived from a planet in the "Sirius constellation" 12,000 years ago and settled in the area after crash-landing due to mechanical difficulties.

While there have been claims that the book is a hoax, Agamon only admitted to it in 1998 during an interview with Fortean Times. However, after personally investigating the matter and reading the book, I found that those who allege it to be a hoax may not have read it in its entirety, given its rarity due to a short print run. I noticed numerous cultural references in the book that were not known in the 1940s or even the 1970s, when the memoir was published, which would have been difficult to research without direct access to Bhutan and Tibet, as Robin-Evans had. Additionally, the book contains references to scientific phenomena and technology that were not yet discovered or invented at the time.

What is Sungods about? Let's explore a summary of the book.

Back in 1978, David Agamon published the memoirs of his employer, Dr. Karyl Robin Evans. The book was written at

Dr. Evans' request on his deathbed. However, in various online versions of the story and in the UFO Files episode, Dr. Karyl is referred to as Carol, despite the clear Germanic spelling of "Karl". This is yet another potential research error or misdirection in the Dropa story and timeline.

The book "Sungods in Exile" tells the story of Evans and his encounter with his colleague, Professor Lolidoff, in 1947. Lolidoff had just returned from Missouri India with a "plate" he had purchased from nomadic Tibetans, which he called the Dzopa. The plate featured a central sun and glyphic writing spiraling out from it, along with depictions of a squirrel, a yoni, a naked humanoid, two spiders or octopus, or even sperm penetrating an egg, and a chameleon. Intrigued by the plate, both men believed it to be an ancient fertility disc from Tibet.

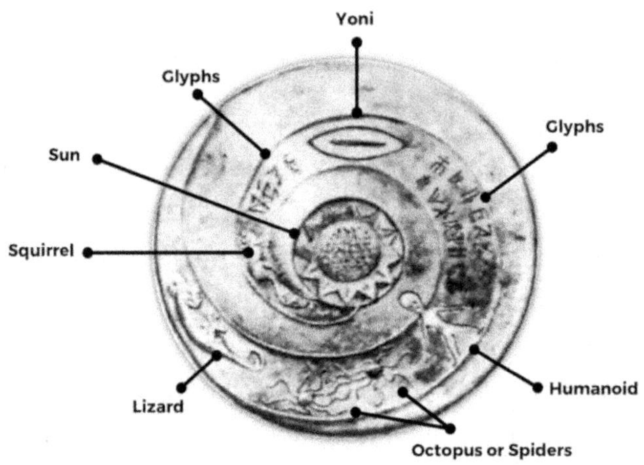

Depiction of the Lollidoff Plate, Sungods in Exile, 1978

Evans became captivated by the story and decided to travel to India to find the Dropa people. He books passage to India, hires a guide and porters to take him through the Himalayas to Lhasa Tibet. While crossing the high passes in Nepal, he encountered a naked meditating monk high up in the mountains seemingly unaffected by the altitude or cold. He also was passed on the trail by a porter traveling at a great speed who was carrying a heavy load about four to five times his weight. Skeptics have doubted the authenticity of these feats, but they are actually possible, as demonstrated by modern-day porters in Nepal who can carry loads up to five times their weight while beating tourists to their destinations, often barefoot or wearing flip flops. As they have a component in their DNA that allows them to acclimatize quickly, they often surprise tourists, who are winded easily but trekking at such altitudes. We also have the amazing physical feats of Wim Hoff who has mastered what the Tibetans call the inner fire, as he is able to meditate for hours in the freezing cold altitudes and the freezing waters of glaciers. While such abilities were not widely known in the 1940s and 1970s, they are now recognized as genuine phenomena.

Nepalese Sherpa carrying a refrigerator usually full of beverages (~500lbs)

Wim Hof meditating on a glacier

Evans ventured into Lhasa, Tibet, where he spent some time learning the language before hiring a guide and a few porters to take him to the Bayan Kara Ula and Bayan Har Shan Mountain ranges in Eastern Kham Tibet, where the Dropa/ Drokpa people lived.

Upon reaching the Dropa valley, Evans was abandoned by his guide and porters. He encountered short, well-armed Dropa guards who initially stopped him. Evans explained that he came in peace and wanted to meet their leaders and learn their story and history. The guards eventually accepted Evans into the village, where he met the rulers Hueypah-la and Veez-la (in my opinion also known as Champa-la and Yeeshi-la, respectively). Skeptics have questioned the authenticity of their depiction in the book, as the only images available are drawings, showing the man wearing a folded robe and the woman wearing a satellite-like hat. However, these styles were common in Eastern Tibet during that time period, and even influenced some of the hair styles and costuming of Queen Amidala (Padmé) from "Star Wars: Episode I – The Phantom Menace," (1999).

Padmé Amidala in costume inspired by Tibetan and Mongalian royal outfits

Both men and women would wear folded wool and silk robes called Chubas, and women would often braid their hair up into wooden or bone scaffolding, depending on their social status, which may appear strange to outsiders.

Depiction of Tibetan Men, 1940

Depiction of Tibetan Women, 1940

Following his introduction to the village rulers, Evans is introduced to Luren, a young woman who serves as his translator. She teaches him the Dropa language using his base understanding of Tibetan and sign language. The Dropa language is a gendered language similar to Spanish or Thai, with a royal tongue and a common basic tongue similar to Shina Brokskat or Brokkat. After learning the language, Evans meets with the Matriarch of the village and then with a nobleman named Lorgen-la, who agrees to share the story of the Dropa with him.

According to Lorgen-la, around 22,000 BC, the space-faring civilizations of the Sirius Star system were involved in a cosmic war that resulted in the destruction of an inhabited moon through nuclear bombardment. After a period of peace, the type 2 civilization scientists collaborated to build great arcs or generational sleeper ships, 2-3km in length, cigar-shaped crafts, and set off to explore nearby stars for inhabitable planets that they could eventually colonize.

Around 12,000 years ago, the Dropa generation ship arrived in our solar system and discovered Earth, a planet like their own home world at Sirius. They sent out exploration ships to collect samples of air, water, minerals, plants, and animals for further study back home. However, during their mission, they were attacked by primitive humans, resulting in the death of some of the Dropa and the capture of others. The young Dropa warriors also engaged in forced sexual intercourse with the beautiful but primitive women of Earth.

Upon returning to the Sirius star system, the Dropa scientists performed tests on the materials brought back and discovered that the humans had similar genetic markers to the Dropa. They concluded that the humans were possibly genetic cousins, and after reading the mission logs, they suspected that there might be a Dropa-human hybrid population on Earth.

In order to find out if there is a hybrid civilization of humans and Dropa on Earth, the Sirius civilization dispatches a smaller, faster generation ship to Earth, which arrives in 1040 AD. They launch a satellite into polar orbit (interestingly the Black Knight satellite is said to have been placed in polar orbit around this time) to spy on the more advanced race of humans and to discover if there is a Dropa-human hybrid population. However, the ship malfunctions once it enters the gravity well of Earth, and the young Dropa warriors mutiny against the matriarchal hierarchy and female pilots of the ship. They find themselves unable to regain control of the ship, so they launch an exploration vessel back to Sirius in hopes of rescue in several generations. Meanwhile, they crash the ship in the remote regions of Tibet and are forced to send out exploration parties to find food and shelter. As some of the parties do not return, it is my opinion that these missing Dropa are the ones found in the caves by Chi Pu Tei and his team. The Dropa eventually trade their precious metals from the craft with the local Kham for seeds, livestock, land, and shelter. Over time, they blend in and interbreed with the Tibetans, adopt their language and religious practices, and become part of the local community.

In 1908, a craft is observed in orbit for several months, but it disappears without landing or sending a rescue vehicle. A few months later, news of an explosion in Siberia spreads, coinciding with the Tunguska event, in which a 40-meter object explodes in the air, flattening more than 20 kilometers of remote forest.

Upon hearing these historical accounts, Evans expresses disbelief and requests to see the ship and the main hall of the monastery in the village, a massive building that stretches for about one kilometer in length and several hundred meters in width and height. He witnesses technology that was unknown to the 1940s, including curved flat screen consoles and fiber optic-like devices for transferring and storing data on disks like modern-day solid-state hard drives. The inclusion of these technologies in the book seems anachronistic since they were not invented until the mid-1980s.

Feeling overwhelmed and shaken by what he has learned and seen, Evans realizes that he has impregnated his translator, Luren, as the Dropa culture is described as very promiscuous to preserve their heritage. Fearing for his life, that of his unborn child, and Luren's, he hastily gathers supplies and his horse and flees westward, never to speak of this story again. On his deathbed, he entrusts his diary and memoirs of his time with the Dropa to his secretary, with the instructions to publish them.

The UFO community claims that this story is a hoax, citing many details that appear fabricated. However, I believe that only a few people have actually read the book, and many rely on the blurb on the back cover. In 1998, someone claiming to be David Agamon confessed to Fortean Times that he had hoaxed the book, which became a major reason for calling it a hoax. Yet, no concrete evidence other than the magazine cover has ever been presented. To verify this claim, I searched for the Fortean Times publication from 1998 that allegedly featured the tell-all article by the supposed author.

THE TIBETAN ROSWELL

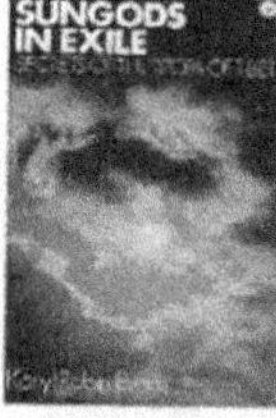

Sungods in Exile (Neville Spearman, 1978) is the account of English anthropologist Karyl Robin-Evans' expedition to northern Tibet in 1947, where he encountered a strange hybrid tribe, called the Dzopas, who claimed descent from the survivors of an ancient crashed UFO. The narrative was edited by David Agamon (who inherited Robin-Evans' papers) and included a photograph of a curious disc-shaped 'plate' embossed with pictograms that seemed to be part of a record of the journey of the star-beings from their homeworld. The author, David Gamon, admitted to *FT* recently that it had been written as a satire on the 'alien intervention in human evolution' genre. Still, it is regarded in some quarters as an authentic 'ancient astronaut' event ***[FT75:57]***.

Fortean Times, #109, 1998

In my search for more information, I also came across the 1998 Fortean Times, #109 publication and hoped to find the alleged tell-all article. However, all I found was a brief 122-word column in the back of the magazine summarizing the Sungods in Exile story and mentioning that the author had claimed it was a fake in a 1994 edition #75 of the publication. It reads as follows:

The Tibetan Roswell. Sungods in Exile (Neville Spearman) is the accuont of English anthropologist Karyl Robin-Evans' expedition to northern Tibet in 1947, where he encountered a strange hybrid tribe, called the Dzopas, who claimed descent from the survivors of an ancient crashed UFO. The narrative was edited by David Agamon (who inherited Robin-Evans' papers) and included a photograph of a curious disc-shaped 'plate' embossed with pictograms that seemed to be part of a record of the journey of the star-beings from their homeworld. The author, David Gamon, admitted to FT recently that it had been written as a satire on the 'alien intervention in human evolution' genre. Still, it is regarded in some quarters as an authentic 'ancient astronaut' event [FT75:57]

SUNGODS IN CUCKOO LAND

My favourite hoax will always be *Sungods in Exile: Secrets of the Dzopa of Tibet* by Karyl Robin-Evans PhD, who explored their mountain fastnesses and revealed how that race has survived poorly there since their mother ship crashed many years ago. This book was published by Neville Spearman 13 years ago and republished as a paperback by Sphere. The author of this leg-pull received correspondence about it from as far away as Kiev. Don't ask me how I know.

David Gamon
Bristol

Fortean Times, #75, 1994

I then tried to locate this 1994 edition but only found a 79-word column describing the book as fake, supposedly written by someone who knew the author, David Gamon. It reads as follows:

Sungods in Cuckoo Land. My favorite hoax will always be Sungods in Exile: Secrets of the Dzopa of Tibet by Karyl Robin-Evans PhD, who explored their mountain fastnesses and revealed how that race has survived poorley there since their mother ship crashed many years ago. This book was published by

Neville Spearman 13 years ago and republished as a paperback by Sphere. The author of this legpull received correspondence about it from as far away as Kiev. Don't ask me how I know.
David Gamon, Bristol

In my opinion, these snippets only serve to create more confusion and do not provide any substantial evidence to support the claim that the book is a hoax.

Moreover, it seems highly unlikely that someone would go to such great lengths to invent scientific technology and have a deep understanding of Buddhist and Bhutanese culture, which were not easily accessible during the 1940s and 1970s. The book's inclusion of such cultural references, scientific phenomena, and technology that were not yet known or invented at the time suggests that the majority of what was written about could be real. While the author, as stated in the book's forward, may have sensationalized some information, it is my opinion that the book holds significant value and should not be dismissed as a hoax.

In my research, I discovered that my findings contradict the claims made by the researchers in the 2004 UFO Files documentary. It appears that they did not conduct sufficient research and were provided with a biased and exaggerated story by their producers, which has influenced every subsequent retelling of the story, including many blog posts, articles and even the Wikipedia entry. Furthermore, I am convinced that the process of transliteration is a significant factor in the misinterpretation and subsequent misdirection of this story, and its claim as being a hoax. Allow me to explain why.

Transliteration, What is it?

Transliteration is the process of converting one writing system into another based on phonetic similarities. It involves hearing a pronunciation in one language and then attempting to write it down in another language. However, this approach can lead to a lot of errors, as some languages have sound formations that cannot be transcribed. As a result, words may be approximated or shortened to make sense in the new language.

The Dropa Stones story originally came from Chinese and was translated into German, then Russian, French, and other European languages before finally being translated into English. With this many translations and phonetic differences, there are likely to be some errors.

In my opinion, most of the names in the original Dropa stories are affected by transliteration.

Let's start with the name "Dropa". As we will see, it is spelled differently depending on the cultural group and changes as you go further west. It originates from the nomadic peoples of Kham, eastern Tibet and becomes "Dzopa", then "Drokpa" and later "Brokpa", all with similar pronunciation depending on who is speaking the name.

The archaeologist, Chi Pu Tei, does not have a Chinese name. I believe that, because he was a master and teacher of his trade, "Chi Pu" is a transliteration of the title "Shifu" or "teacher". Looking up the last name "Tei", I discovered it is a direct transliteration of "Teochew", a Chinese surname from a province in eastern China. Therefore, the archaeologist would have been known as "Shifu Tei" or "Master/Professor/Teacher Tei" as a professional title and a name of respect for his students. It is possible that most of the

Dropa researchers did not consider or research transliteration or other possible pronunciations of this or other names in the story, as they all refer to him as a fictional character.

Moving on to another name affected by transliteration, we have Professor Tsum Un Nui, which is also not a Chinese name. During the early 20th century, there were many Hao Chinese/Vietnamese mixed individuals who were involved in teaching and the sciences.

It is possible that Tsum Un Nui is a transliteration of the name "Tsuong or Troung Nguyen", a common name for individuals with Chinese and Vietnamese heritage during this time period.

Another instance where transliteration has caused confusion is in the naming of the tribes mentioned in the original German article from 1964. While the original article clearly refers to the Kham tribes of Tibet, later translations have referred to them as the Ham Chinese. However, based on the original materials and the region the story comes from, it is my opinion that the "Ham" actually refers to the Kham Tibetan people of this region.

It is important to note that there is no tribe of Chinese origin called the Ham, but there is a dynasty called the Han, which has a very different lineage.

Traditional Kham Tibetans, wearing Chubas and women with braided hair in bone or wood scaffolds, 1940s

It is also worth considering the history of the Kham Tibetan people, who were trained by the CIA to become spies and assassins during the Chinese Invasion and occupation of Tibet. The people of this region of far east Tibet, where the Bayan Kara Ula and Bayan Har Shan mountains are located, are also known as Khampa or the people of Kham. However, their involvement in espionage during the 1950s has made their history difficult to uncover.

By applying transliteration to the story presented by the UFO Files researchers, it alters the course of the investigation and provides new paths to explore. Instead of searching for Chi Pu Tei, the focus should be on locating Shifu Tei. However, this task is challenging since the Beijing Academy of Sciences and Prehistory, where Tei supposedly worked, was re-established in 1949 as the Chinese Academy of Science in Beijing, and Mao's Chinese revolution in 1966 resulted in the destruction or concealment of many records and historical information.

Instead of investigating the Dropa people, attention should be given to the Drokpa and Brokpa, who are also nomadic yak herders and high-altitude farmers. Although I attempted to obtain blood samples from them around 2005 when my father was guiding tours in Bhutan, he was not willing to allow bloodletting during his tours. Consequently, I was unable to obtain any DNA evidence of their possible extraterrestrial origins if they exist.

Regrettably, a significant portion of the Chinese history leading up to the mid-1960s, along with archeological finds, cultural documents, research, music, instruments, art, and sculptures were destroyed during Mao's Chinese Cultural Revolution. This movement aimed to erase all of China's history before 1966. It was a dark period as one of the oldest cultures on Earth underwent a forced purification, leading to the destruction or concealment of many artifacts. We may never learn what happened to the original stones, mummified bodies, research papers, or any other discoveries related to the Dropa lore and legend, except for what could be smuggled out of China in the years leading up to the event. Furthermore, we do not know the fate of the disks sent to the Soviet Union for further examination in the early 1960s since the storyline appears to halt following the scientific and mineral testing and oscillation testing.

We need to also consider the issue of transliteration when analyzing the Sungods in Exile story, as a few of the names involved in this story also bear the signature of mispronunciation.

A Look at the Information We Do Know

Initially, the artifacts were discovered in remote caves. These caves were known to contain incredible artifacts, as evidenced by the discovery of many other caves in the region, dating back thousands of years, and verified through carbon testing of organic materials. Some of the caves in the Bayan Kara Ula range contained ancient Petroglyphs, some dating back over 6,000 years, and depicted pyramids, or bricked and layered rays of the sun. Others contained depictions of hunters dancing around the sun of Sirius, accompanied by dogs and other animals, or a Sungod with an angry face and outstretched arms. One wonders if this is a representation of a solar outburst.

Many other caves in the region, such as those found in Tarim, contained mummified bodies that were remarkably preserved due to the arid climate of the area. These bodies had skin that was golden yellow in color, often with golden strawberry blonde hair and blue or green eyes. It's worth noting that Genghis Khan was described as a golden-skinned, blue-eyed, redheaded person and not of Chinese descent. While most of this region was part of ancient Tartaria, red and auburn hair and blue-green eyes were common features of the local population.

Finally, the caves in Dolpo, Nepal, dating back 14,000 years, held religious artifacts, scrolls, documentation, and paintings that predate both recorded history and modern Buddhism. Given all of this, it is logical to assume that Shifu Tei was searching for cultural artifacts and ancient burials in this ancient land.

It is fascinating to note the presence of the Kham Tibetans, also known as Khampa, in the region of Tibet where the artifacts were found. The name Khampa is similar to the Champa of Cambodia, which is researched by David Hatcher Childress. This name is also associated with ancient Egypt, known as Khem. These transliterations are believed to refer to the same people and ancient culture, which share a common history, religious beliefs, and even megalithic structures with key-stone cuts found across the globe. It is possible to connect the Kham of Tibet, the Cham of Cambodia, most famous for the enigmatic temple structures of Angkor Wat, and the Olmec of Central America through the Sanxingdui culture found near Kham Tibet, which is also shrouded in mystery.

Large face sculptures and temple structures of Angkor Wat, Cambodia, 900+ years old

The Sanxingdui and the Olmecs

The Sanxingdui culture is undoubtedly one of the most fascinating recent discoveries in China. While it is currently believed that the culture existed around 1000 BC, its distinctiveness from other Chinese cultures of the time has led some to question whether it might be older than previously thought. The Sanxingdui people inhabited a region near the eastern border of Kham Tibet, close to the Bayan Kara Ula Mountain ranges as well as the enigmatic Chinese pyramids and terracotta warriors.

The Sanxingdui archaeological site is located in China's Sichuan province and was discovered in the 1920s. However, it was not until 1986 that its significance was fully recognized. The site is believed to have been part of the ancient Shu civilization and dates to the Neolithic period, around 3,000 years ago. The two large sacrificial pits found at Sanxingdui contain a vast collection of artifacts, including pottery, bronze objects, jade pieces, and masks, which were used in religious ceremonies. These artifacts display intricate designs and advanced metallurgy techniques, such as lost-wax casting. The discovery of the Sanxingdui site has challenged previous assumptions about ancient Chinese civilizations and raised questions about the Shu civilization's relationship with other ancient Chinese cultures, such as the Zhou and Qin dynasties. The artifacts found at the site suggest that the Shu civilization had a sophisticated culture and advanced metallurgy skills, previously unknown to researchers.

It is fascinating to note that the large-format bronze and copper sculptures found at the Sanxingdui site exhibit a unique and somewhat enigmatic art style that appears alien to modern viewers. However, upon closer examination, similarities have been observed between the Sanxingdui artifacts and those of the Olmec culture in Central America. In fact, some artifacts even feature ancient Shang dynasty glyphs, suggesting that there may have been some connection or exchange of ideas between these two distant cultures. The discovery of such connections challenges our understanding of ancient civilizations and highlights the need for further exploration and research in the field of archaeology.

Asian features on an Olmec Jade Mask

Asian features of an Olmec Statue

Olmec Statue

While there is no widely accepted evidence of a direct connection between the Olmec civilization of Mesoamerica and ancient China, some researchers have suggested possible links between the two cultures based on similarities in artifacts, such as jade carvings and pottery, and the possibility of early trans-Pacific voyages. One hypothesis proposes that ancient Chinese seafarers may have traveled to the Americas as early as 5,000 years ago, potentially bringing advanced knowledge and technology that influenced the development of Mesoamerican cultures like the Olmecs. While the theory remains controversial, there is an artifact, Offering 4 from La Venta, Tabasco, that suggests a connection between the two cultures. The artifact comprises 16 human figures with six celts, made from jade, serpentine, and granite - materials commonly used in China at that time. Interestingly, the back of the pillars of this small sculpture group features ancient Chinese Shang (Sanxingdui) culture glyphs.

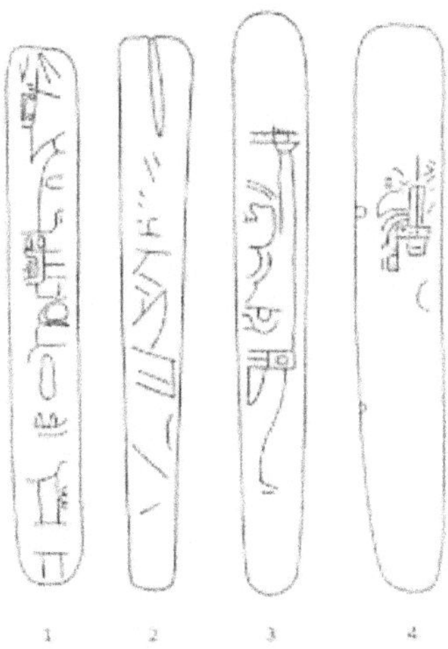

Offering 4 from La Venta, Mexico

Despite some researchers pointing out similarities between Olmec and Chinese artifacts, it has been suggested that these similarities could be explained by cultural diffusion, which could have facilitated the exchange of cultural and technological innovations through trade and communication networks. It is known that trade routes existed between Mesoamerica and Asia, including China, during the pre-Columbian era.

Currently, there is no solid evidence to support claims of a direct connection between the Olmec and ancient China. While some theorists have suggested a possible link, the similarities between the two cultures could be attributed to cultural diffusion or coincidence. Further research is needed to fully understand the relationship between these two ancient civilizations.

Ancient Shu or Sanxingdui bronze statue, similar to Olmec statues, 1180 BC

Tartaria the Unknown Empire

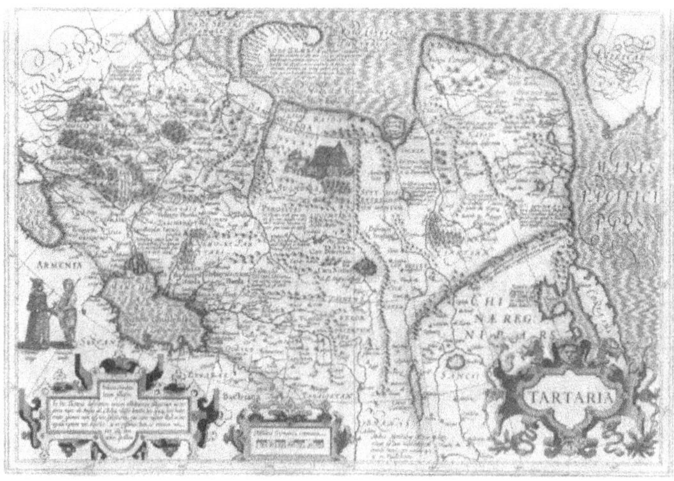

Ancient Tartarian Map

Tartaria was a vast land that spanned across Japan, Russia, China, Mongolia, Kashmir, and Central North Asia, extending into Europe and beyond. Its legacy is mostly evident in the uniformity of its architecture. The people of Tartaria were described as fair-skinned, red-haired, and blue-green-eyed, and the empire is said to have reigned for a long period. Though few ancient maps still depict Tartaria, some books and movies mention this old time, such as the Ian Fleming James Bond Novel "You Only Live Twice" and Michael Crichton's "Eaters of the Dead." The Soviet Union attempted to erase any records or relics that could provide a history of Tartaria when it was formed, despite occupying much of the empire's territory. The Great Wall of China remains shrouded in mystery, as some believe it was built to fend off the barbarians or Tartarians, but in reality, it protects the Tartarian empire to the west and acts as a barrier against the Chinese empire to the east.

The Dropa Cave in The Bayan Kara Ula Mountains

14,000-year-old cave in Dolpo, Nepal

The cave itself is also intriguing due to its supposedly impossible hewn construction out of bedrock into straight cut walls, floors, and ceilings. However, a similar cave with a wall hewn out of bedrock to a perfectly flat surface within 1/1000 of an inch can be found in Peru at Nappua Iglesia. This cave is located on a hillside in the Sacred Valley between Ollantaytambo and Machu Pic'chu and has almost 90-degree angle cuts in the corners and an alcove with three levels of relief detail, all perfectly cut and aligned.

The technique used to create such a cave is unknown and applies to other similar sites found worldwide, such as the giant rooms at the Petra site in Jordan, the Barabar caves in India, the Lonyou caves in China, and the cave that *Shifu Tei* allegedly stumbled upon in the Bayan Kara Ula range of far east Kham Tibet. The question remains: what was the technique used to cut such precise and detailed structures?

Friend and researcher Brien Foerster at Nappua Iglesia cave, Sacred Valley, Peru, and its dimensions

Barabar caves in India, 300 BC+

Lonyou caves in China, possibly 1552–1667 AD, but perhaps much older

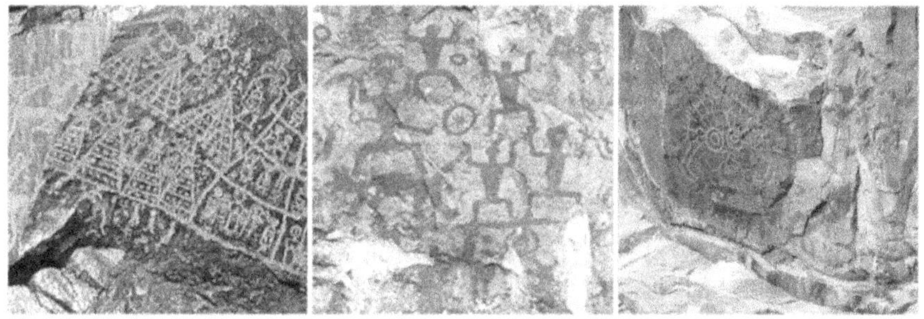

Chinese petroglyphs found in the Bayan Kara Ula area of China

The presence of petroglyphs in the cave is not unusual, but the combination of these rock carvings with the cave and its contents creates a mystery. In the rear of the cave, there are rows of mummified and skeletal remains. While the Tarim mummies have been preserved for several thousand years, it is uncertain whether this particular site is 6000 years old or older, or even more recent, as we learned from the story of the Sungods in Exile.

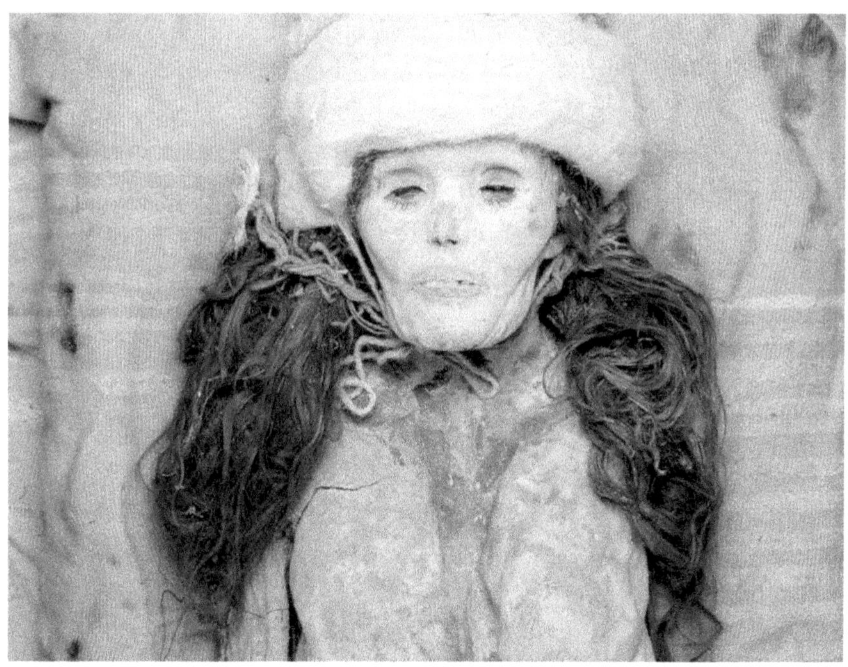

6000-year-old Tarim mummies with auburn hair and blue green eyes

Examples of the enigmatic Bi disks from China

The disks found in the cave may have engravings of an alien race, but the story told on at least one of them is from the perspective of observers of a crash or landing, not the Dropa themselves. The disks resemble Bi disks, which were often buried with noblemen, priests, or rulers, possibly beings thought to be deities on earth, perhaps Sun gods? Most disks are blank and made from granite and jadeite materials, while a few are decorated with magic, spells, curses, geometric shapes, stars, and other motifs. Although the meaning of the disks is unknown, there is one that has come down through Chinese legend and lore, known as the Emperor's Jade Seal.

Examples of the enigmatic Bi disks from China

The Emperor's Jade Seal

Depiction of the Emperor's Jade Seal

The Emperor's Jade Seal was a highly esteemed and mystical artifact that was passed down among the ruling lineages until it vanished during the Ming dynasty between 1368 and 1644 A.D. Among the various renowned Chinese seals and Bi disks, the Heirloom Seal of the Realm, also known as the Emperor's Jade Seal, stands out as the most prominent. This seal was created in 221 BC out of the Heshibi jade Bi disk, a stone that, according to legend, cost one man his feet. The seal symbolized the Mandate of Heaven, a concept used to legitimize the rule of the Emperor of China, who was believed to embody the natural order of the universe and referred to as the Son of Heaven. This sacred relic was passed down from emperor to emperor until it mysteriously vanished sometime between 908 and the Ming Dynasty.

In contrast, the Dropa stone inscriptions are described as being on only one disk out of the reported 716 found. The disk, about a foot wide with a central hole and two spiraling lines, bears a glyphic language unknown to Shifu Tei and his team when they discovered it in 1938. The engravings are said to be visible only under a magnifying glass, indicating they are very small, which raises questions about the ability to engrave such intricate details on Jadeite or other granites. While India and Egypt show examples of sophisticated engravings, they tend to be on a larger scale.

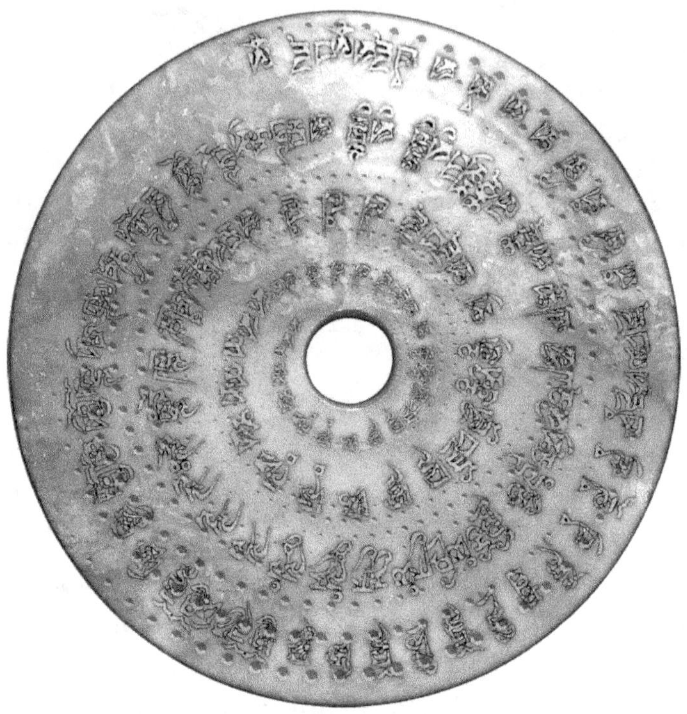

Author's depiction of a jadeite disc with spiraling glyphic writing similar to the description of the Dropa stone

Etching of Jadeite and Other Hard Stone

Jadeite with cobalt and mercury infusion

It appears that etching text into jadeite-cobalt stone is not impossible, but the level of detail that can be achieved depends on the micron size of the stone. Even with modern laser engraving techniques, it is not possible to achieve extreme detail on such a small scale. The granular matrix of the stone causes it to crumble under heat and pressure, and jadeite is composed of small micron grains of granite and larger micron grains of crystal. Any cutting or engraving method used would have to account for the different microns and adjust its tolerance as it moved along. A laser engraver was consulted and confirmed that cutting on stone can be done, but not with extreme detail if the size is below a certain threshold.

"It could be possible if it is a polished stone, we could probably engrave it. The problem is when you are engraving an unknown material you need to do some testing to get the correct settings. So, if the piece is expensive, you might ruin one before you get it correct. Would it be possible for someone to make one from clay and fire it as an easier alternative?" ~David

It is true that laser etching technology was not available in ancient China and was only invented in the 20th century. As you mentioned, the first laser etching/engraving machine was used in 1978, long after the Tsoung Nguyen translation of the Dropa stones in 1958. Therefore, it is highly unlikely that the ancient Chinese could have etched such small and intricate scripts on a jadeite-cobalt stone.

Examples of laser engraving and acid etching on stone, metal and glass

It is also worth noting that the materials listed, such as metal, glass, resin, and porcelain, have a much smaller micron size (a unit of length equal to one millionth of a meter; a micrometer) compared to jadeite-cobalt stone, which makes it easier to etch smaller scripts. These materials can be etched using acid etching or laser engraving technologies, which were not available in ancient times.

The Alien or Foreign Writing on the Disks

Depiction of Chinese, Tibetan, Shina / Brokskat and Kham Tibetan writing

The writing on the disks presents a second anomaly. While it is described as "alien," the term alien can also refer to something *foreign* and unknown to Professor Tsoung Nguyen. It is possible that the disks were written in a very foreign glyphic writing system such as Kham Tibetan, which is vastly different from Chinese characters, given their location of discovery in Kham Tibet. Another possibility is that the writing on the disks could be an older language of Shina origin, such as Brokskat or Brokkat. Without a cipher or base language, Tsoung Nguyen would not have been able to attempt a translation of a foreign or alien script. However, if the writing was in Kham Tibetan or Shina, which could have been found throughout the region, he would have had the foundation needed to make a translation within a few years, as described. Interestingly, Tsoung Nguyen dated the disks to 12,000 BC, but carbon dating was in its infancy during this time, having been discovered only 8-10 years earlier. Additionally, it is not possible to carbon date stone, only organic materials can be carbon dated. It is intersting to discuss the dating of the organic materials taken from the cave, and my thoughts on how the burial might be newer than previously thought, circa 1040 AD based on the revelations of a return voyage of the Dropa during this time, when they actually crashed their craft. The organic materials and perhaps clothing remains could be from a much older lineage, as the craft, crew and thus clothing originated from Sirius around this time, still appearing new and not degrading over the course of approximately a few thousand years, due to the use of generation sleeper ships, and thus hybernation technologies, which are discussed later on in this book.

Depiction of Dropa cave burial circa 1040AD or earlier

Mineral and Oscillation Testing on the Disks

HP Oscillating testing machine of the 1960's

The final segment of the story revolves around the disks ending up in Russia, and how Soviet scientists obtained one or more of the disks during the same time period that Professor Tsoung Nguyen was translating them. It remains a mystery as to how they acquired the disks.

It is said that the scientists removed some materials from the disks to conduct a mineral analysis. The results were stunning, revealing the presence of jadeite, cobalt, and another metal, which was likely mercury as it is often found in jadeite samples. Both cobalt and mercury are conductive metals and can hold a charge. Jadeite, being a crystalline-based stone, can create a piezoelectric effect under intense pressure.

Piezoelectricity is the accumulation of electric charge in certain solid materials such as crystals, ceramics, and biological matter like bone, DNA, and various proteins in response to applied mechanical stress. If the disks were part of an apparatus or under physical stress, they would create a charge that could be held by the cobalt and mercury present in the disks. This is similar to how modern cellphone and electric car batteries work, which are made of a crystal salt, lithium, combined with cobalt and sometimes mercury.

It is unfortunate that the fate of the disks after the tests performed by the Soviet scientists is unknown. It is possible that they kept the disks, or they were returned to China, but with Mao's cultural revolution already underway, their whereabouts may never be known. The fact that the disks were able to create a charge and pulsing rhythm through oscillation testing suggests that they had been around charged electricity for some time and retained a base charge. It is interesting to note that Christopher Dunn discusses piezoelectricity and rhythmic electrical pulsing as part of the mechanism that came from the power plant of the Great Pyramid at Giza in Egypt, although this was not known at the time of the Dropa stone tests in the Soviet Union in the late 1950s to early 1960s.

Carbon 14 Dating and Timelines

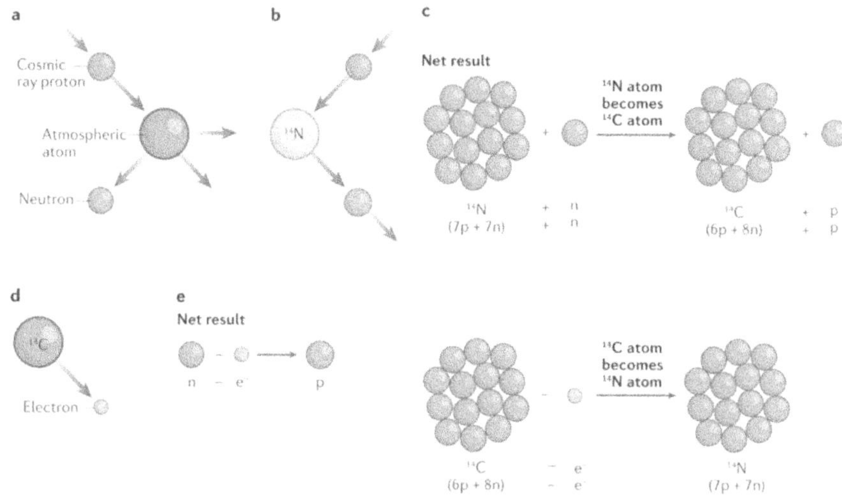

Example of radiocarbon 14 dating

Radiocarbon dating is a method used to measure the age of objects containing carbon-bearing material by detecting the decay of a radioactive isotope of carbon (14C). With a half-life of 5,700 ± 30 years, radiocarbon dating can be used to date specimens formed over the past 55,000 years. This Primer outlines key advances in 14C measurement and instrument capacity, as well as optimal sample selection and preparation. However, it's important to note that although the original 1938 story carbon dates the Dropa stones to roughly 10,500 BCE, carbon dating was not discovered until the mid-1940s, and it is not possible to carbon date stones, only organic materials.

Additionally, one of the embellished stories surrounding the Dropa stones describes bodies found with enlarged heads on small frames, yellow skin, and blue eyes, suggesting a burial much more recent than 12,000 years old, possibly from 1040 AD when the Dropa returned. However, without surviving documents from the excavation, it is impossible to know the true age of the burials.

The enlarged heads and small bodies could also be attributed to the presence of dwarves in the region, with their skin becoming yellowed and leathered over time due to exposure to the elements.

Kham Tibetan with rare blue eyes

It's important to be aware of the cultural and historical context surrounding the descriptions of the alleged Dropa people. Racist tropes and stereotypes have often been used to dehumanize and marginalize groups of people, and it's crucial to approach any such descriptions with a critical eye. Additionally, it's worth noting that physical features such as eye color and skin tone are not necessarily indicative of a person's ancestry or cultural identity.

The Search for Shambala

Helena Blavatsky, who founded the Theosophical Society, claimed to have been contacted by the Masters of the Ancient Wisdom who reside in Shambala. She wrote extensively on the subject, describing it as a hidden city in the Himalayas and a center of spiritual power and wisdom.

Nicholas and Helena Roerich, a Russian couple who were spiritual seekers and artists, also believed in the existence of Shambala and conducted expeditions to find it. They traveled throughout Central Asia and Tibet in search of the hidden city, and their experiences were chronicled in the book "Shambhala: In Search of the New Era."

Alice Bailey, another prominent figure in the Theosophical movement, also wrote about Shambala and its role in the spiritual evolution of humanity.

In modern times, there are still those who believe in the existence of Shambala and seek to connect with its energy and wisdom. It remains a mysterious and elusive concept, steeped in mythology and spiritual lore.

Madame Blavatsky, a Theosophist, traveled to India in the late 1870s in search of ancient wisdom and secrets from India, Nepal, and Tibet. She discovered the Great Brotherhood of Light, also known as the White Brotherhood, and the Ageless Wisdom tradition and mysteries of Shambala through her interactions with Djwhal Khul, a Tibetan monk and practitioner.

Djwhal Khul, an ascended master and guide to Madame Blavatsky, channeled many of Alice Bailey's books in the early 20th century. He taught about the effects of the Sirius system on our world, and when asked about the primary cause of the world crisis during World War II, he cited "a welling up of magnetic force on Sirius, which produces effects upon our solar system and particularly upon our Earth." He asserted that the energies of Sirius stimulated both the best and the worst in humanity, as exemplified by the global conflict, which mirrored a cataclysm that occurred around Sirius thousands of years ago.

Alice Bailey, who succeeded Blavatsky, collaborated with the channeled Djwhal Khul to write 24 books from 1919 onwards about the Great Brotherhood of Light, the secrets of Shambala, and other esoteric teachings published by the Lucis Trust, formerly known as the Lucifer Publishing Company. Bailey believed that the Great White Lodge of Freemasonry was based in the Sirius System, known on Earth as the Great Brotherhood of Light.

In 1924, *Alexandra David-Néel* also traveled to Tibet in pursuit of magic, mystery, and Shambala with her guide *Yongden*. She became the first Western woman to enter the city of Lhasa and learned a great deal about these subjects. However, she ultimately concluded that Shambala might be entered in northern Afghanistan near the city of Balkh, which is located on the Drokpa/Brokpa nomadic trail to the Black Sea.

Nicholas Roerich, a visionary artist, and idealist, embarked on a journey to Tibet between 1923 and 1928 in search of Shambala and the legendary Cintamani Stone. It has been suggested that Roerich was commissioned by future US President Franklin D. Roosevelt, a 33rd degree Free Mason, to find the stone. While there are claims that Roerich successfully reached Shambala and was gifted the stone by the monks, such assertions are questionable as it is unlikely that the Buddhists would readily part with one of their most sacred artifacts. Instead, it is possible that Roerich was given a piece of a meteor from a similar time period and origin as Sirius, similar to the Kaaba stone in Mecca and the Chinga meteor found in Mongolia, as was the case with the Buddhist Iron Man.

While these ideas are certainly intriguing, it's important to approach them with a critical and open mind. Many of these concepts are based on mythology, legend, and speculation rather than concrete evidence. While it's possible that there are ancient and mysterious artifacts or places that have yet to be discovered or understood, it's important to approach these ideas with caution and skepticism until there is more evidence to support them. It's also important to acknowledge the cultural and historical context in which these ideas emerged, and to recognize the potential for bias and prejudice in the way that these stories are told and interpreted.

The Tibetan Buddhist Iron Man

The Buddhist Iron Man is a significant artifact associated with the Sirius system. It is an iron statue of a Buddhist deity, likely Vaiśravana, which was brought from Tibet to Germany by a German expedition in 1938-39. This statue is believed to have an extraterrestrial origin and was possibly created from a fragment of the Chinga meteorite, which fell in the border region between Russia and Mongolia around 10,500 BC. This is the same time period as the Holocene comet event and the dating of the archeological Dropa cave findings from 1938, as well as the fall of Atlantis according to Plato.

The Iron Man statue is estimated to be around 1000 years old, and metallurgy was known in China and Tibet during that time. It features a swastika symbol, which was likely a factor in its appeal to the Germans, who twisted and usurped the symbol for their own purposes. The statue also has a unique geometric patterned body armor and, most notably, holds the Cintamani stone in its hand.

Japanese Sirius Zen Legends of Utsuro-Bune (The Mystery of the Hollow Ship)

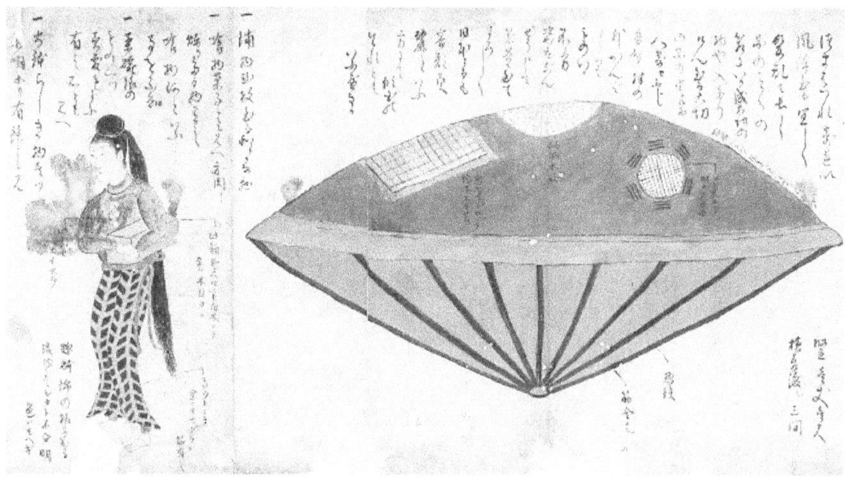

Utsuro-Bune (The Mystery of the Hollow Ship)

In 1803, a peculiar vessel drifted ashore in Hitachi province. The craft was round, equipped with rigging and ridges, metal-plated, and featured crystal glass windows submerged in resin. A mysterious woman, standing at just 4ft 5in with auburn red hair, emerged from the craft. She spoke in an unknown language and wore unfamiliar clothing while clutching a strange box. The box bears enigmatic glyphs that resemble symbols discovered at the sites of the Roswell UFO crash in 1947 and the Bentwaters UFO incident in 1956, leading some researchers to speculate that the vessel may be an escape pod from a ship hailing from Sirius.

Further, some researchers suggest that the box may be a traditional Japanese decapitated head box or Kubi-Oke, while others propose that it could be the enigmatic box from Sirius that houses the four gifts: the Cintamani Stone, the Vajra Dorje, the Buddha's Singing Bowl, and the Ohm Mani Stone.

Buddhist Astrology, the Sirius Chinese Astrological Coin

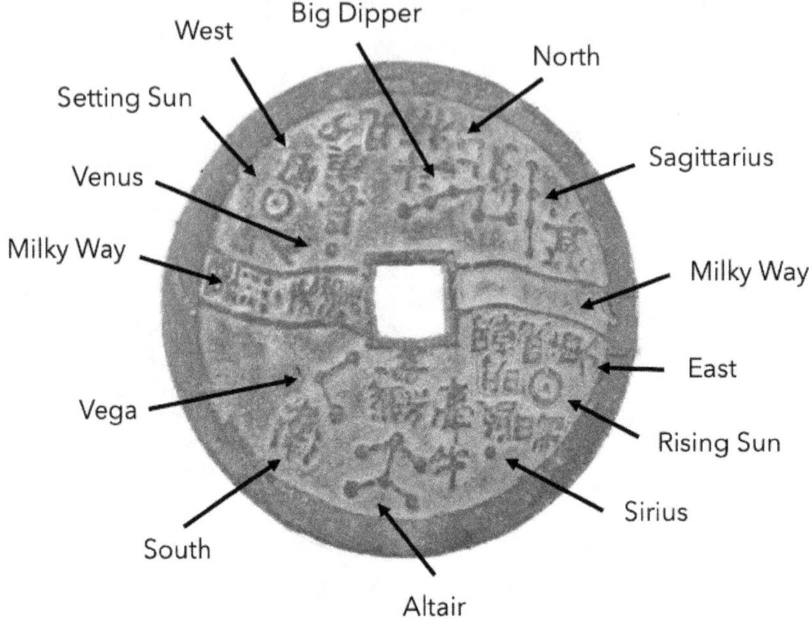

The depiction of Sirius rising in the East can be found on ancient Chinese astrological coins dating back to the Han dynasty, around 25 BC. One such coin was discovered in the city of Xian, and similar coins have been found from different eras of Chinese history. These coins suggest that the Chinese were observing the stars and were aware of the importance of Sirius in their astrology and astronomy. The depiction of Sirius rising in the East was likely significant in their beliefs and practices and may have played a role in their agricultural and religious calendars.

The Golden NASA Discs

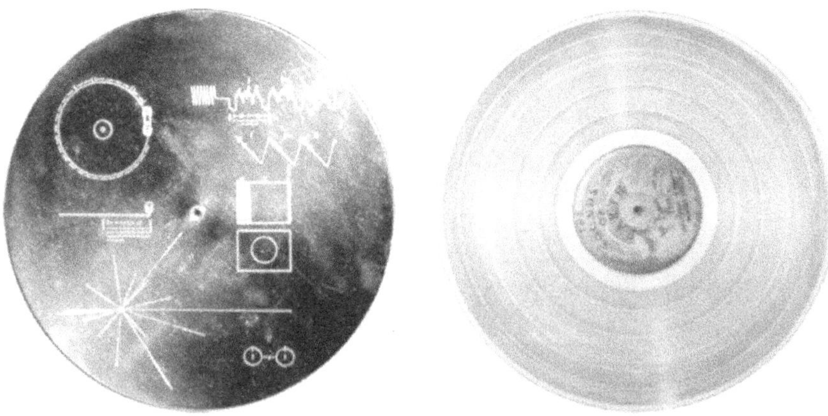

The Voyager golden disks, NASA, 1977

NASA launched two Voyager spacecraft in 1977, each carrying two 12-inch discs made of gold and electroplated with pure uranium-238. The half-life of this element is around 4.5 billion years, which makes it suitable as a time capsule for potential extraterrestrial discoveries. The cover of the discs displays a triangulation of the location of the Sun and Earth based on our observations of pulsar star configurations. It also includes a representation of the chemical makeup of Earth, universal mathematical constants, and instructions on how to play the record stored within the covering.

The record contains images, music, sounds, and greetings in various modern and ancient languages, including Wu Chinese, a language over 3000 years old. The discs come with a photo and phonographic player and specialized diamond-tipped needle, along with more iconographic instructions on how to use them. The glyphs and spiral grooves on the Dropa stones bear some similarities to the iconography used on the NASA discs. However, the glyphic writing on the Dropa stones is believed to be of Kham Tibetan or an older Shina-Brokskat script.

EXPLANATION OF RECORDING COVER DIAGRAM

THE DIAGRAMS BELOW DEFINE THE VIDEO PORTION OF THE RECORDING

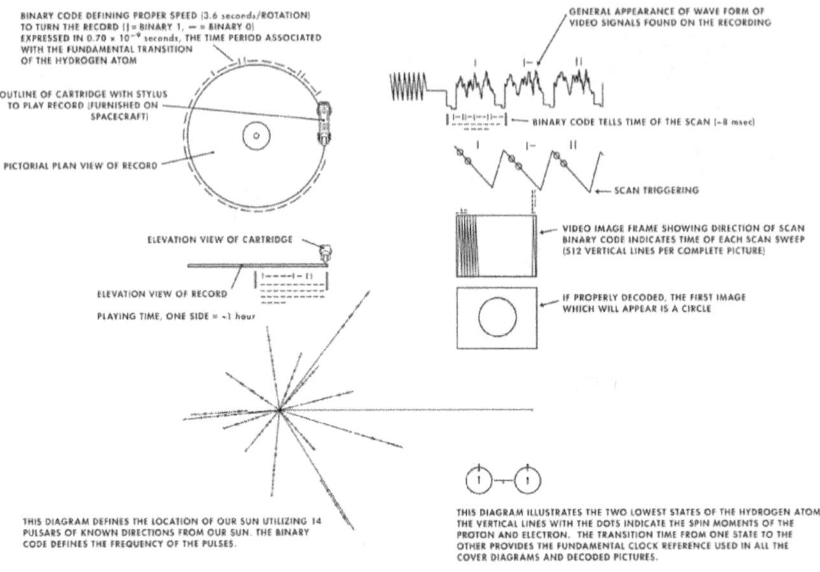

Testing the Voyager golden disks, NASA, 1977

Tibetan UFOs, Magic and Contact

https://www.youtube.com/watch?v=U8Ibolcw8dw

Let us embark on a journey back to Dharamsala, North India, in 1992. It was there that an intriguing conversation took place between Harvard psychiatrist John E. Mack (1929-2004) and the Dalai Lama, centered around the topic of extraterrestrial beings. Mack was no stranger to the subject of aliens, having dedicated years to researching individuals who claimed to have had experiences with them in North America. His work primarily revolved around understanding the phenomenon of alien abductions.

Surprisingly, it seemed that the Dalai Lama was knowledgeable about aliens as well. During the conversation with Mack and a small group, the Dalai Lama conveyed that he believed aliens to be sentient beings within the vast universe. He also shared Mack's belief that these entities were initiating contact due to their concerns about humanity's detrimental impact on the environment.

Several years later, in 1999, Dr. Mack had another opportunity to meet with the Dalai Lama in Dharamsala, India, where they participated in a symposium focused on world peace.

During this visit, Mack conducted an interview in which he discussed his observations regarding the Dalai Lama and his perspective on aliens. According to Mack, highly esteemed Tibetan lamas like the Dalai Lama, who resided at a level of profound mystical consciousness, were unlikely to have dramatic encounters or abductions involving aliens. Enlightened beings such as the Dalai Lama were already accustomed to interacting with a diverse range of entities and beings that held significant reality in their cosmic worldview. They embraced a perspective that transcended materialism and Western beliefs, acknowledging that phenomena could traverse from the unseen realm into the material world.

In essence, it seemed illogical for individuals of the Dalai Lama's elevated state of consciousness to undergo the type of transformative and mind-expanding abduction experiences commonly reported by Mack's more ordinary North American research subjects. In other words, the Dalai Lama's advanced level of awareness, which was so distinct and "alien" in comparison to mainstream thinking, rendered encounters with avant-garde alien consciousness redundant. Put simply, the Dalai Lama was already attuned to the wavelength of the aliens.

CIA Declassification of 1960's UFOs Over Nepal, Bhutan and India and the Sightings of the Yeti

It is noteworthy that among the recent declassifications by the CIA, Navy, and US government concerning the topics of UFOs and UAPs, there was also a release about the CIA monitoring reports of UFO sightings and the mysterious Yeti from Nepal, India, and Bhutan. In an opinion piece in the Kathmandu Post, Amish Mulmi discusses the findings from the declassified documents, only to ultimately debunk the stories, as is often the case with mainstream journalists who wish to maintain their credibility. Mulmi also refers to a linked article from the BBC that discusses the infamous Yeti finger, which was purportedly discovered to be human DNA. Many researchers believe that Bigfoot and the Yeti are genetic cousins of humanity, making them hominoids. It is interesting to note that the original finger may have been swapped out for a human finger, which could have been the finger that was stolen all along, in the author's opinion. Nonetheless, the set of articles provides an intriguing read.

How the US Kept Tabs on UFO Sightings and Yeti Hunting in Nepal

The Kathmandu Post: Opinion

by: Amish Raj Mulmi • Published: February 8, 2019

https://kathmandupost.com/opinion/2019/02/08/on-ufos-and-yetis

Conspiracy theories on CIA cover-up about extraterrestrial activity aside, the note on UFOs is extremely fascinating.

On 25 March 1968, at 8.15 pm, residents of Batulechaur in Pokhara, on the way to Mahendra Gufa, witnessed an unusual phenomenon. 'A blazing object, flashing intermittently, accompanied by big thunder sound disintegrated over Kaski region.' Although urbanized today, Batulechaur would have been little more than a few homes amid rice fields at the time. Pokhara itself was a sleepy town, centered around the north-south axis of Bagar to Ramkrishna Tole, the old market. The American Central Intelligence Agency (CIA), however, found the phenomenon interesting enough to classify it as an unidentified flying object (UFO) in a report dated 13 June 1974. Most intriguingly, the document noted that 'a huge metallic disc-shaped object with a six-foot base and four feet in height was found in a crater at Baltichaur (sic), five miles NE of Pokhara.'

Is the truth out there?

This was not the only instance of UFO spotting by the CIA in our part of the world. Although the sources have been redacted, presumably for security reasons, similar bright objects were seen in the skies above Ladakh, Thimphu, Sikkim, and Olangchung Gola and Ghunsa in the east of Nepal, where 'a fast-moving object, long and thin, emitting red and green bright light, as bright as to

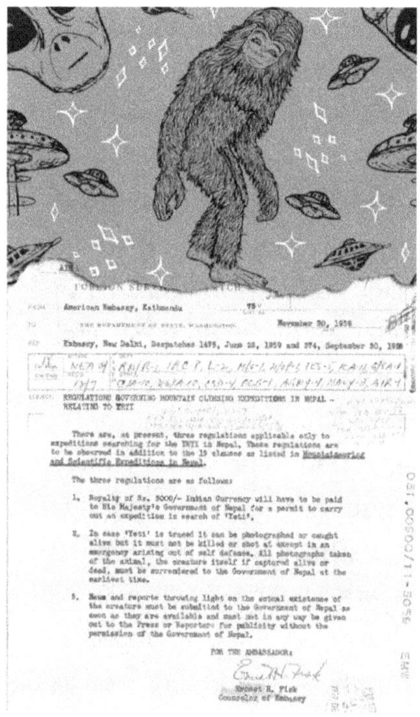

American Embassy, Kathmandu

November 30, 1959

Embassy, New Delhi, Despatches 1475, June 22, 1959 and 374, September 30, 1959

REGULATIONS GOVERNING MOUNTAIN CLIMBING EXPEDITIONS IN NEPAL - RELATING TO YETI

There are, at present, three regulations applicable only to expeditions searching for the YETI in Nepal. These regulations are to be observed in addition to the 15 clauses as listed in Mountaineering and Scientific Expeditions in Nepal.

The three regulations are as follows:

1. Royalty of Rs. 5000/- Indian Currency will have to be paid to His Majesty's Government of Nepal for a permit to carry out an expedition in search of 'Yeti'.

2. In case 'Yeti' is traced it can be photographed or caught alive but it must not be killed or shot at except in an emergency arising out of self defence. All photographs taken of the animal, the creature itself if captured alive or dead, must be surrendered to the Government of Nepal at the earliest time.

3. News and reports throwing light on the actual existence of the creature must be submitted to the Government of Nepal as soon as they are available and must not in any way be given out to the Press or Reporters for publicity without the permission of the Government of Nepal.

FOR THE AMBASSADOR:

Counselor of Embassy

cause daylight' was seen on the night of 19 February 1968. The document covers UFO sightings between February–March 1968, during which there were seven such sightings in these areas.

The report is part of a trove of documents the CIA declassified and released in 2017. As expected, the archives focused on Nepal cover Cold War geopolitics, American preoccupation with Communist presence in Nepal, Sino-Soviet aid, and Indian outlook towards the country. There are also notes about the early days of democratic Nepal. A 3 January 1950 note reads, 'Many of the ruling Ranas [...] are purchasing property outside of Nepal... They fear the Communist menace which is mostly indigenous.... Congress party members seem to be operating in concert with the Communist party against the government'. In 1953, after the flight of K.I. Singh to China, a CIA note read: 'In early November 1953, K.I. Singh was staying in a village near Tradum [Tibet]... where the Chinese Communists had established for him a headquarters where he could organize and train Nepalese Communists.' A footnote adds, '[redacted] in April 1952 Dr. Kaiser Indra Singh [sic]'s followers in Tibet were being trained by Chinese Communist Army officers. Notably, none of the archives related to Project ST Circus, the CIA covert operation that trained and inserted Tibetan Chushi Gangdruk guerrilla fighters into Tibet via Mustang and other upper-Himalayan regions, has been released.

The note on the UFOs is short. There aren't any explanations provided, or if there are, they've been redacted. Extraterrestrial explanations aside, could the sightings simply be countries testing out new surveillance aircraft? The CIA suggested the agency was itself responsible for 'reports of unusual activity in the skies in the 50s'; turns out they had been testing the U-2 high-altitude reconnaissance aircraft secretly. In a report that declassified the development of the U-2 program, it said the aircraft could fly up to 73,600 feet, and 'access to the photographs...would be strictly controlled.' One assumes inter-departmental secrecy meant those who drew up the UFO sightings note did not know about the U-2 flights until much later. From the report's conclusions, it is clear that testing of the new aircraft resulted in several sightings from across the world. 'High-altitude testing of the U-2 soon led to an unexpected side effect – a tremendous increase in reports of unidentified flying objects...once U-2s started flying at altitudes above 60,000 feet, air-traffic controllers began receiving increasing numbers of UFO reports,' the highly redacted report reads, 'U-2 and later OXCART (another high-altitude spy plane) flights accounted for more than one-half of all UFO reports during the late 50s and most of the 1960s.'

We cannot say what the 'huge metallic disc-shaped object' that crashed in Batulechaur was, since we don't know what happened to the remains. If it were a part of the aircraft, one would assume US authorities would have gathered it. There aren't any other declassified reports about UFO sightings from our part of the world, although other reports count sightings from Sweden, Denmark, West Germany, and Turkey.

Conspiracy theories on CIA cover-up about extraterrestrial activity aside, the note on UFOs is extremely fascinating. It tells us about the agency's breadth of coverage in a country, especially because Nepal at the time was largely remote, with little or no transport infrastructure to speak of. How did the information from Olangchung-Ghunsa—which remains difficult to reach even in the modern day—reach US authorities?

However, this was not the only instance of the X Files playing out in Nepal. On 30 November 1959, the American embassy in Kathmandu sent out a memo to the State Department about the Himalayas' best-kept secret: the Yeti. The memo curiously outlines three regulations 'applicable only to expeditions searching for the Yeti in Nepal'. A background blog suggests the regulations had been issued by the Nepal government 'two years before' and then translated to English, and it makes for an irresistible read.

Yeti 'Hunters'

Photo of alleged Yeti footprint, Nepal, 1951

The first of the regulations stipulated any expedition to look for the Yeti would have to pay a royalty of INR 5000 to the government. If the Yeti was found, 'it can be photographed or caught alive, but it must not be killed or shot at except in self-defense.' Any photographic evidence, or if the Yeti was caught alive or dead, was to be submitted to the Nepal government. Also, any news or reports about the Yeti could not be released to the press without permission from the government.

But where the note gets interesting is the background blog that suggests even though the US government did not believe in the existence of the Yeti, 'the memo was instead a strategic move to demonstrate the US support of Nepal sovereignty.' Nepal's position as a strategic buffer between India and China, two countries the US wasn't particularly close to at the time, meant the US needed a presence in the country so that it could monitor the two, as well as Soviet influence in the country. However, 'both India and Nepal were wary of Western imperialist nations, but the US needed Nepal's approval to maintain an embassy within Nepal's border and—on a larger scale—they needed India's political support in the region.' The memo was a signal that the US diplomatic presence in Nepal was 'entirely non-threatening'.

The backgrounder's explanation is quite unsatisfactory. After all, US presence in Nepal also served to soothe the nerves of a Nepali establishment already wary of overreaching Indian and Chinese influence at the time. The two neighbors had, in any case, entered into treaty agreements by the date of the memo recognizing Nepal's sovereignty. A memo on Yeti hunting would not satisfy the two neighbors about the US's 'non-threatening' presence.

However, if we consider the idea that the memo had been issued at a time when western 'explorers' were scouring the mountains for signs of the Yeti, it makes more sense. The most (in)famous of these explorers was Peter Byrne, who headed a 1957 expedition funded by Texas oil millionaire Tom Slick. On Slick's instructions, Byrne nicked a finger from the famous Pangboche monastery hand, which purportedly belonged to a Yeti, in 1958. Although Byrne, who was most recently sentenced for fraud in the US, later said the monks allowed him to take a finger after he made a donation of Rs.10,000 to the monastery, an Everest summiteer who started a campaign to 'return the hand' to the monastery suggests Byrne got a monk drunk and stole the finger. 'While the monk was passed out with a tummy full of scotch, Peter cut a finger off from the original Yeti hand and replaced it with a human bone. The monks were none the wiser.'

Whatever the truth, what was clear was that the finger was illegally smuggled to the UK, another relic that joined the list of artifacts smuggled from Nepal to the private collections and museums of the west. The Pangboche hand has now been proven to be hominid in origin, and perhaps the mystery of the Yeti itself has already been debunked [see BBC.com article] to more unremarkable explanations, just like the UFOs.

End of Article.

Yeti finger mystery solved by Edinburgh scientists

Published: 27 December 2011, BBC.com

https://www.bbc.com/news/uk-scotland-edinburgh-east-fife-16316397

The mystery of a yeti finger taken from Nepal half a century ago has been solved with the help of scientists at Edinburgh Zoo.

The mummified remains have been held in the Royal College of Surgeons Museum in London since the 1950s.

A DNA sample analyzed by the zoo's genetic expert Dr Rob Ogden has finally revealed the finger's true origins. Following DNA tests, it has found to be human bone.

The yeti, also known as the Abominable Snowman, is a legendary giant ape-like creature said to inhabit the Himalayan region of Nepal and Tibet.

Despite the lack of evidence of its existence, the yeti myth retains a strong appeal in both Nepal and the west, where it became popular in the 19th century.

The finger, which was said to be from a yeti, was taken from a Nepalese monastery by an American explorer in the 1950s.

He replaced it with a human finger he had been given by a British scientist.

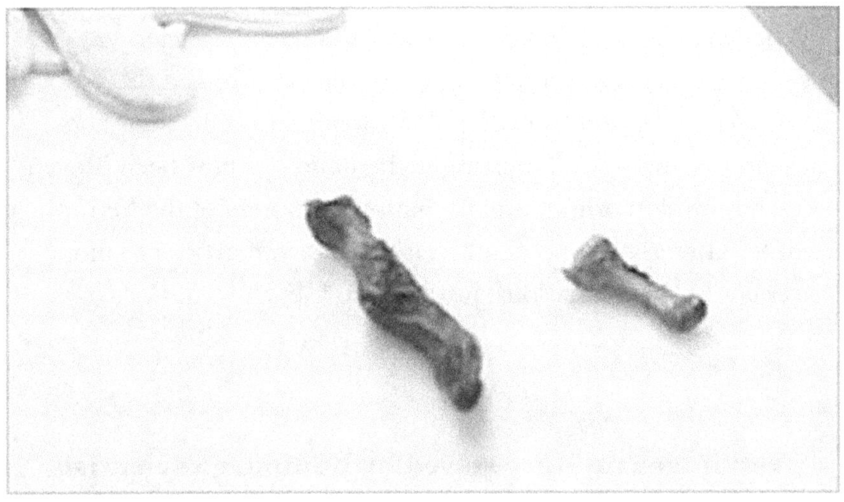

The yeti finger taken from a Nepalese monastery by an American explorer, 1950s.

It was then smuggled out of India with the help of Hollywood actor James Stewart, who hid the artefact in his wife's lingerie case.

The finger is now held in the Royal College of Surgeons Museum in London.

Just recently it was rediscovered during cataloguing.

They allowed a BBC documentary team to take a DNA sample.

It has been analyzed by genetic experts at Edinburgh Zoo, who concluded it is human.

Dr Rob Ogden, of the Royal Zoological Society of Scotland, said: *"We had to stitch it together. We had several fragments that we put into one big sequence and then we matched that against the database, and we found human DNA."*

"So, it wasn't too surprising, but it was obviously slightly disappointing that you hadn't discovered something brand new.

Human was what we were expecting, and human is what we got.

Primatologist Ian Redmond said: "From what we know of accounts of Yetis, I would have expected a more robust and longer finger and possibly with some hair on the back.

If one had just found it without the story attached to it, I think you would think it was a human finger."

End of Article.

As previously mentioned, I believe that a large portion of this story may have been fabricated, as it would have been extremely difficult for the actor to replace the Yeti finger with a human finger and smuggle it out of the country without detection by the watchful monks. Additionally, the monks would not have sold the finger to Peter Byrne, as it is still on display, and they would have noticed the differences in appearance and size. Even if Byrne had managed to trek out of the Khumbu region undetected, he would have eventually been caught.

I have personally seen the Yeti finger and scalp during a trek in the Khumbu region when I was 13 years old. The finger closely resembles the Denisovan finger that was discovered and is considerably larger than an average human finger (18cm versus an average of 6.5cm), with mummified skin and hair. It is unlikely that any human, aside from a tall basketball player, would have fingers of such a size, certainly not Nepalese, Tibetan or "Bear".

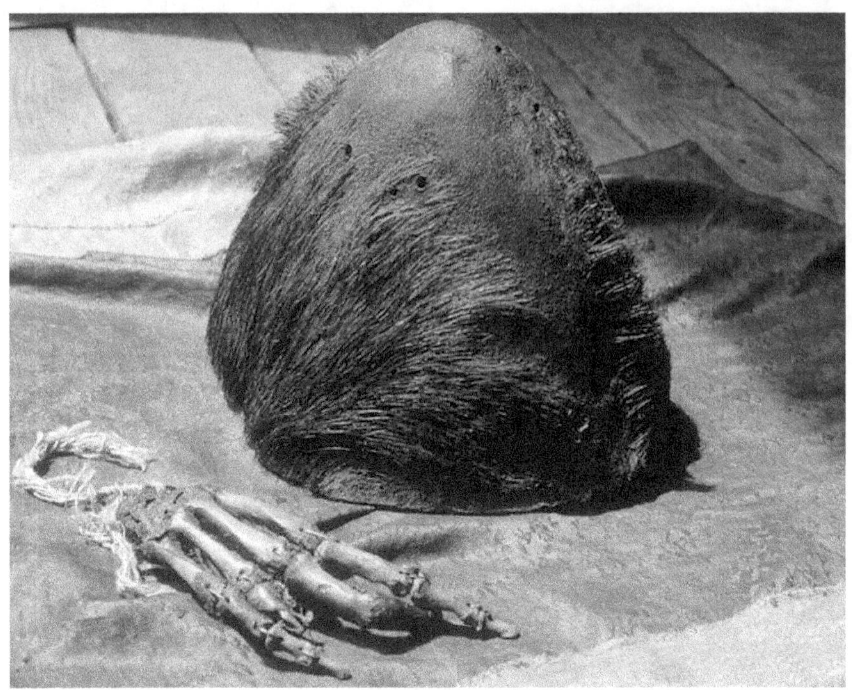

Photo of the alleged Yeti scalp and hand

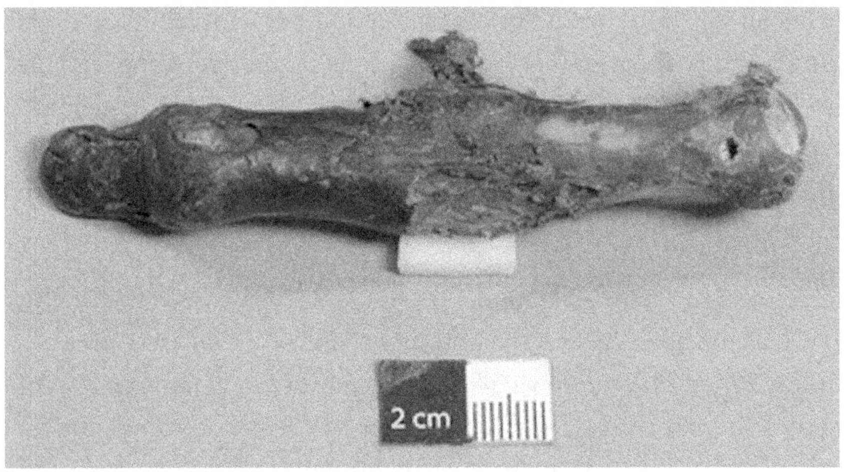

Photo of the alleged Yeti finger and measurements

In my view, the finger that was swapped for the alleged Yeti finger was actually a human finger all along, which was then taken to England for analysis. The late researcher Lloyd Pye believed that the Yeti and Bigfoot were hominoids and genetic cousins of humans, and in the 1950s, it would have been difficult to distinguish their DNA. Moreover, there are no scientific reports or findings available on this matter, except for the BBC report, which seems to be eager to dismiss this story as a hoax and mislead researchers into believing it. I think it would be fascinating to uncover the truth behind this story, but since all the people involved in it have passed away, it will remain an unsolved mystery in my research.

Depiction of the Chinese Yeti, called the Yeren or "wild man"

Yeren depicted above the entrance at Shennongjia Forestry District, China

An Introduction to Generation Ships

Generation ships are a common theme in science fiction, often depicted as long-haul sleeper ships shaped like cigars, designed to transport colonies to far-off worlds that are too distant for a crew to reach using sub-light speeds. To survive the journey, the crew must either enter a state of hibernation or hyper sleep or breed successive generations to take care of the ship and its passengers. This concept has been explored in many modern science fiction movies, including "Star Trek 4: The Voyage Home" (1986), "Event Horizon" (1997), "Pandorum" (2009), and "Avatar" (2009).

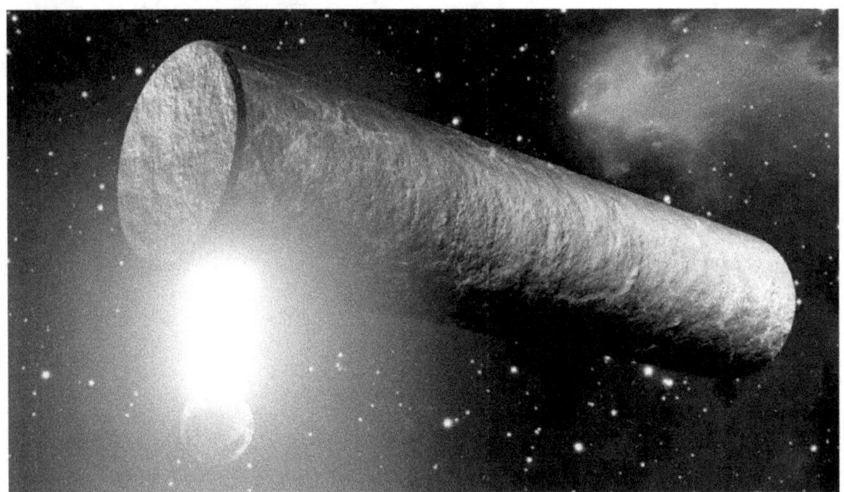

Space probe seen in Star Trek 4, The Voyage Home, 1986

Avatar Interstellar Vehicle (ISV), Avatar, 2009

Chris Pratt and Jennifer Lawrence star in "Passengers" (2016), which also features a generation and hibernation ship. The Alien franchise movies are known for their use of hibernation ships, including the Nostromo in "Alien" (1979), the USS Sulaco in "Aliens" (1986), and the colony ship in "Alien Covenant" (2017), among others. Even "Prometheus" (2012) includes a similar concept.

USS Sulaco, Aliens, 1986

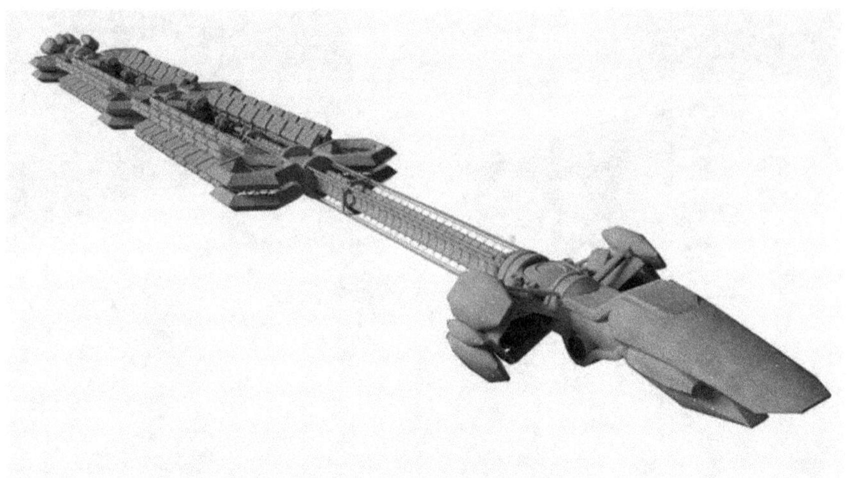

Colony Ship, Alien Covenant, 2017

These ships typically come from civilizations that have not yet discovered faster-than-light or FTL drives, warp speed, wormhole travel, or hyper drives like those depicted in the Star Wars and Star Trek franchises. However, the concept of a Generation Sleeper Ship was introduced in the 1967 Star Trek Original Series episode featuring the S.S. Botany Bay, in which Captain Kirk finds Khan Noonien Singh and his crew in suspended animation (hibernation) after leaving Earth in the 1990s.

S.S. Botany Bay, Star Trek Original Series, Space Seed, 1967

The Battlestar Galactica (1978 to 2004+) could also be considered a type of Generation ship, although it does have an FTL (faster than light) drive.

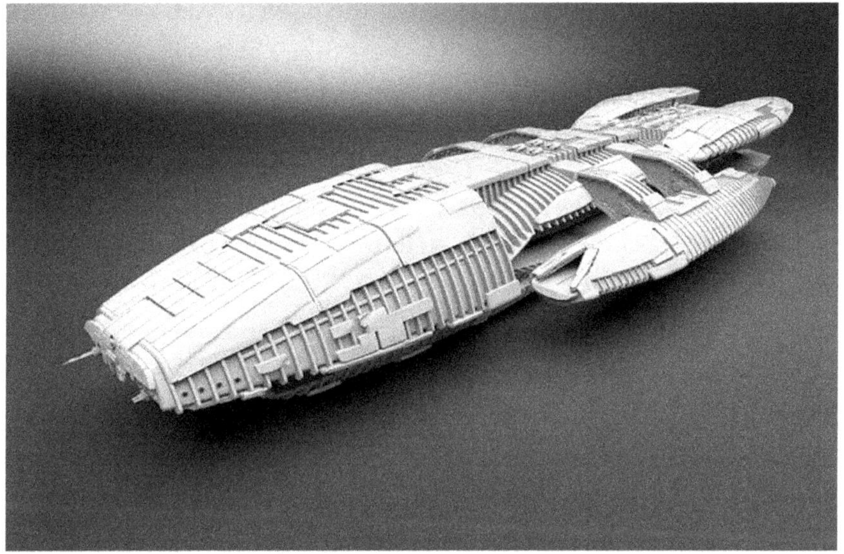

Jupiter class Battlestar Galactica, 1978 - 2004

In the book "Sungods in Exile", it is mentioned that the Dropa crash-landed on Earth in a cigar-shaped Generation ship approximately 1 km in length, which took around 5,000 years to travel from Sirius, going about 650 times slower than the speed of light. Based on the timelines in the story, this would be equivalent to approximately 10 generations for the Dropa, or at least 3 generations based on suspended animation or hyper-stasis.

Yes, the concept of generation ships and hibernation or sleeper ships has been a popular theme in science fiction movies for decades. These movies often explore the psychological and physical challenges that arise when people are forced to live in confined spaces for extended periods of time, as well as the ethical and moral questions around bringing new life into the world under such circumstances. Some movies also delve into the technical aspects of such long-haul space travel, such as the maintenance of life support systems, propulsion systems, and the need for resources and supplies to sustain a population over many years or even centuries. The popularity of these movies may reflect our ongoing fascination with the idea of exploring the universe and colonizing other planets, as well as our awareness of the challenges and risks involved in such endeavors.

It is fascinating how a recent space event has sparked numerous discussions. Arthur C. Clarke's groundbreaking book "Rendezvous with Rama," published in 1973, tells an exciting story set in 2130 about an interstellar object approximately 50km long and 30km wide, tumbling and discovered passing Earth enroute to the sun. In a summary, a crew, including Simps (synthetically modified chimps) that work efficiently in space, is dispatched to intercept it. As Rama gets closer to the sun, it starts to slow down and come online. The crew is inside when this happens and has various thrilling survival adventures, including interacting with tri-pod robotic creatures and discovering a flower, a signal of life. As Rama reaches the gravity of the sun, it changes directions and speeds up to slingshot to another part of the galaxy.

Oumuamua, an Interstellar Object

Depiction of Oumuamua, an interstellar object discovered in 2017

In 2017, the Haleakalā High Altitude Observatory on Maui made an extraordinary discovery: the first observed and tracked interstellar object, meaning it originated from beyond our solar system. Dubbed Oumuamua, roughly translating to "scout" in Hawaiian, it was tracked for about 4 months as it made its way towards the sun after passing by Earth. Similar to Rama, the interstellar object in Clarke's book, Oumuamua is tumbling at an incredible speed of 196,000 miles per hour (87.3 kilometers per second) while measuring approximately ½ to 1 km in length, 10 times as long as it is wide, and having a cigar shape. Although it is often reported as being around 400-500 meters in length, it's unclear why there is such a discrepancy. As it passes Mercury, it slows down, likely due to the sun's gravity, which would have captured its mass. However, it then changes direction and speeds up, as if using the solar gravity to sling shot itself around the sun and off to another part of the galaxy.

This unusual behavior has puzzled scientists and astrophysicists alike as it doesn't act like a comet or show any signs of off-gassing, and it certainly doesn't have the profile of an asteroid. According to Avi Loeb, an astrophysicist and plasma physicist, as well as a professor of science at Harvard, the characteristics of Oumuamua are more like that of a spacecraft or something intelligently driven. The name "scout" is particularly fitting. The tumbling of a cigar-shaped object at such high speeds in space would create an artificial gravity on and within the object if it were hollow. Additionally, the fact that it slowed down in the sun's gravity and then changed direction, as well as surfed the gravity to increase speed to slingshot around the sun, suggests an object that is intelligently driven, potentially by beings, AI, or a combination of both.

While it's certainly an intriguing possibility, it's important to keep in mind that there is currently no concrete evidence to support the idea that Oumuamua is a spacecraft or that it is related to the Dropa stories in any way. While its unusual behavior has puzzled scientists, there are still many other possible explanations for its characteristics besides the idea that it is artificially constructed and intelligently driven. It's important to approach such theories with a healthy dose of skepticism until there is sufficient evidence to support them.

"Oumuamua's appearance in our solar system was a surprise and suggested it had been flung here by some kind of energetic gravitational slingshot — which could be explained by its origins in a binary star system, scientists say."

By Nicole Karlis, Senior Writer, Salon.com

Published 3/21/2017

https://www.salon.com/2018/03/21/oumuamua-came-from-a-binary-star-system-researchers-say/

Depiction of the Chinese generation ship proposed, 2021

The scientific community is abuzz with suggestions about the possibility of Oumuamua being a scout craft from the binary star system of Sirius, possibly here to observe Earth and look for or contact descendants of the Dropa. Coincidentally, in September 2021, China announced plans to construct a Generation-type ship in Earth's orbit, with a length of approximately 1.5 km. The ship is designed for long-term scientific research and could potentially be used for interplanetary and interstellar travel. As a researcher, I find this development fascinating, as it presents two intriguing possibilities for exploration and discovery.

The scientific community is abuzz with suggestions regarding the possibility of Oumuamua being a scout craft from the binary star system of Sirius, here to observe Earth and possibly contact Dropa descendants. In September 2021, China announced plans to build a Generation-type ship in Earth's orbit, which will be roughly 1.5 km in length and will be built for long-term scientific study, interplanetary and interstellar travel. As a researcher this is fascinating as there are two possibilities based on the research conducted.

The first possibility is that China may have back engineered the technology of the crashed Generation ship found in the Bayan Kara Ula mountains when they invaded Tibet in 1950 and are now building something new in secret or collaboratively. This is speculation, but China's biotech and computer science industries are currently leading in creating circuits, chips, and cold storage, among others. It could be a Manhattan project of sorts, with various projects being compartmentalized, and those deemed failures become black projects.

The second possibility is that China found something interesting on the back side of the moon with the Yutu 2 lander and robotics. China has led several successful space missions to orbit, the moon, and even Mars.

In my research into cigar shaped Generation ships I cannot help but think of a 2005 online discovery discussing secret NASA missions to the back side of the moon and the discovery of a derelict space craft.

Vimanas on the Moon, a High-Octane Speculation

2005 Depiction of "Mona Lisa on the Moon" and Guest Crater photographed by Apollo 15, 1971

In the summer of 2005, I came across a Hindi blog discussing ancient Vimanas on the moon while researching blog reports and videos online. I was particularly interested in this topic due to my previous exposure to Vedic scholar and alternative archaeology researcher Michael Cremo's work. The Mahābhārata, a story of Gods, Demigods, and humans fighting in flying palaces and cities using Brahmāstra weapons, fascinated me. The weapons were described as emitting blinding light and burning the lands around their detonation points, killing fleeing animals. Although the story was written around 300 BC and reads like poetic science fiction, it is considered the greatest spiritual epic of all time.

The blog post in question discussed what appeared to be a crashed Vimana on the back side of the moon, which was visible in reconnaissance photos taken during the Apollo 10 mission, which only orbited the moon to take photos for potential landing sites. Follow-up photography was conducted during the Apollo 15 mission while awaiting the crew of the Lunar Excursion Module (LEM) on the moon's surface to return to the command capsule.

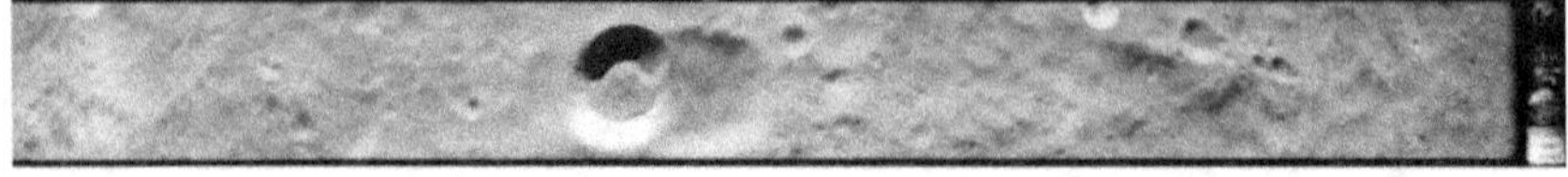

Full spread photo shows detail and is not washed out…

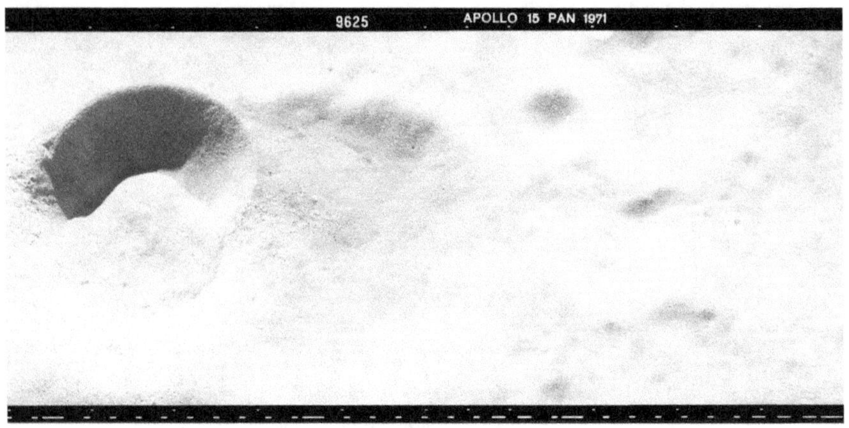

https://wms.lroc.asu.edu/apollo/view?image_name=AS15-P-9625

Contrast and image balanced photo from NASA AS15-P-9625

The photo allegedly shows a large crater called Guest crater, which is about 19km wide and located at coordinates 19.79°S

117.39°E. Interestingly, within the crater, there appears to be what looks like a cigar-shaped craft that has crashed near the rim. However, skeptics have claimed that the photo is a fake produced using photoshop. It's worth noting that NASA released the Apollo 15th photography in July of 2021 for the 50th anniversary, but this specific panoramic of photos, labeled 9625 Apollo 15 Pan 1971, appears incredibly washed out, as if it had been overexposed. Adjusting the brightness and contrast of the photo reveals an image of what looks like a craft, which could be considered photo manipulation, but not photo fakery. Additionally, when searching for Guest crater on Google Moon, it appears to be missing, but it can be found by typing in the coordinates provided by NASA, and the image of the crater is also washed out, with the secondary crater to the east appearing blurry.

Google Moon search for Guest Crater provides no results

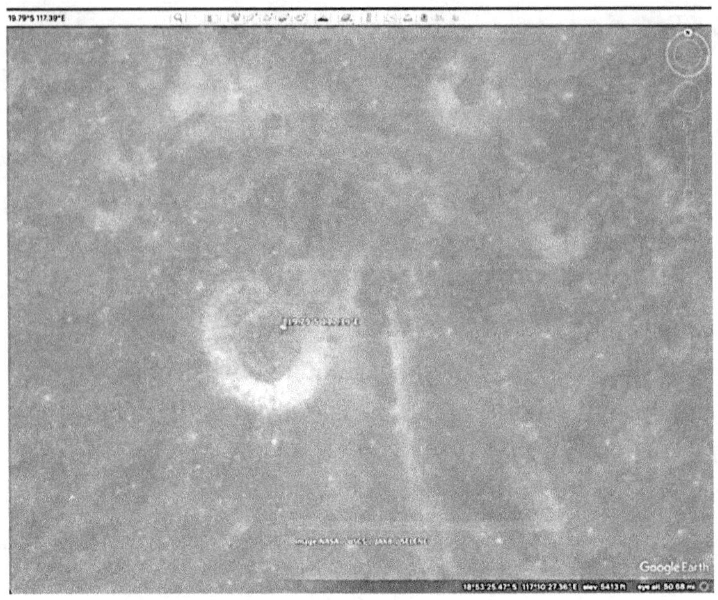

Guest Crater found with NASA coordinates, seems very washed out

In addition to the photograph from Apollo 15, there were four other images. One of them depicted a supposed secret space mission patch, while another showed the inside of an LEM door with an Apollo 20 patch and a picture of a Soviet/USA split flag, suggesting a joint mission that allegedly took place in 1976. The remaining two photos depicted a short, young woman with yellow-golden skin wearing eye electrodes or a HUD (heads-up display) cover attached to her forehead, nose, and mouth with a biomechanical scaffolding. In the last photo, the electrodes had been removed, revealing her blue eyes. Notably, the appearance of the young woman in the photo is similar to descriptions of the Dropa and the physical depictions of young Drokpa women.

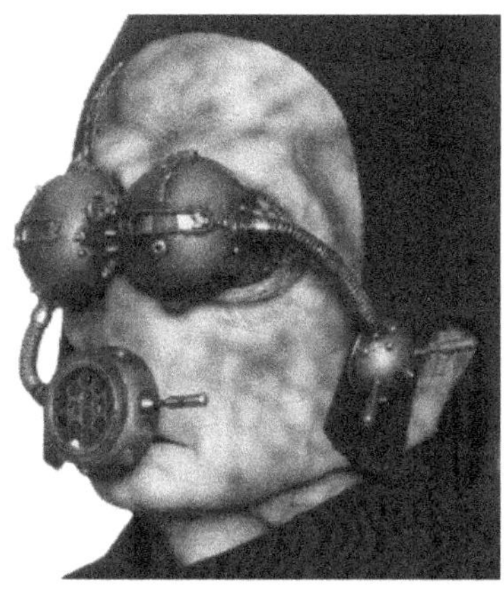

Neimoidian Navigator Star Wars: The Phantom Menace (1999)

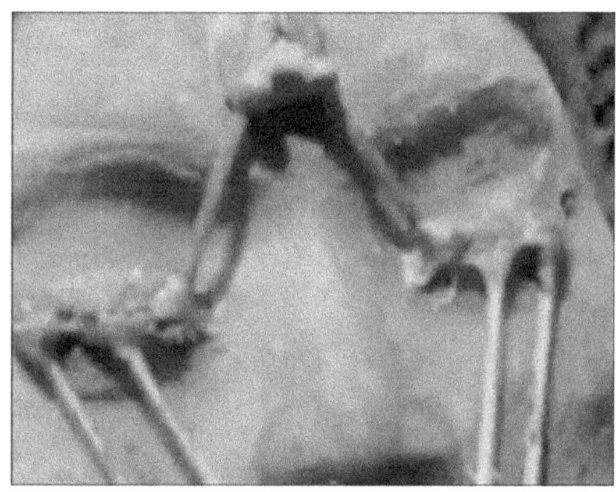

Apollo 20 Mona Lisa, a possible Dropa Navigator

It is interesting to note that a similar concept can be seen in the Neimoidian pilot in "Star Wars: Episode 1 - The Phantom Menace" (1999).

Interestingly, in 2007, this story surfaced on a more mainstream blog (which is also no longer available) and included a couple of low-quality videos showing a flyby of the ship and a recreation of what appears to be the removal of the eye electrodes from the woman in the photos from two years prior. However, this story has quickly been called a hoax for the following reasons:

Firstly, it was apparently an April Fool's Day joke and therefore not a serious story.

Secondly, the Apollo 18, 19, and 20 missions were officially cancelled in 1970 due to budgetary constraints, so these missions never actually existed.

Thirdly, as NASA was a military-controlled "civilian" organization during the height of the Cold War, it is highly unlikely that they would have shared the ultimate "high ground" with their supposed enemy, the Soviet Union, and there would never have been a joint mission or mission flags.

It is important to approach any claims or stories with a critical eye and conduct thorough research before drawing conclusions. While some stories may turn out to be hoaxes, others may have elements of truth that warrant further investigation. It is always important to gather as much information as possible and examine it from multiple perspectives before coming to a conclusion.

Apollo 18, 19 and 20, the Secret Missions

When investigating the claims of the Apollo 20 hoax, I initially focused on the April Fool's Day joke that is often cited as the origin of the hoax. However, the original blog post and release date of this alleged joke are unclear and may not even exist. In 2007, the hoax narrative resurfaced with poor-quality videos and additional photos, but the source of this material is questionable. The hoax gained renewed attention in 2017 with the release of Thierry Speth's book "Apollo 20, the Unknown Mission: Memories of the Commander of the Mission, William Rutledge." The book recounts a fantastical story about the Apollo 18 recon mission, the Apollo 19 discovery mission, and the Apollo 20 rescue mission to a crashed cigar-shaped UFO near Guest Crater on the moon. It is important to approach such claims with skepticism and to seek out reliable sources before drawing conclusions.

Cover art from the 2 Apollo 18, 19, 20 books, 2010, 2017

The book "Apollo 20, the Unknown Mission: Memories of the Commander of the mission, William Rutledge" by French author Thierry Speth was released in 2017, following a resurgence of the Apollo 20 hoax narrative in 2017. Italian author Luca Scantamburlo also published a book in 2010 titled "Apollo 20. The Disclosure" which expands on the supposed Apollo 20 mission and the story of William Rutledge. In an interview with Thierry Speth, he claimed to have hoaxed the original story on April Fool's Day in 2007, but admitted that his props were stolen and he only had a poorly made mask of the alien woman referred to as "Mona Lisa on the Moon." However, given the lack of verifiable information, this claim by Thierry cannot be confirmed.

Interestingly, in 2008, Google and Virgin collaborated to create the company Virgle, which was a predecessor to Virgin Galactic. On April 1st, 2008, Virgle released a public service announcement claiming that water had been discovered on Mars, a claim that has been rediscovered on every Mars mission since Viking first found water in the atmosphere in 1975. It is important to approach all claims with skepticism and conduct thorough research before drawing conclusions.

Here is a brief summary of the April Fool's Day prank that occurred in 2008:

WIRED.com

https://www.wired.com/2008/04/google-and-virg/

Google and Virgin Team Up to Spell 'Virgle'

In about the funniest April Fool's Day spoof I have seen, Google hilariously outlines their new 100 year "vision" to select a group of Virgle Pioneers to start a Plan B civilization on Mars- "The Adventure of Many Lifetimes."

It starts with a 15 question multiple choice quiz to help determine your suitability to be a Virgle Pioneer. It includes questions like, "I am a world-class expert in: a. physics b. medicine and first aid c. engineering d. Guitar Hero II"

So Sergey Brin and Richard Branson have finally teamed up. I can't think of any better way to start the morning or to start a new civilization. They even did their homework and included *real* Mars facts in the FAQ.

If you have ever dreamed of going to Mars, or are in need of a good belly laugh head to www.google.com/virgle.

Update: Larry and Sergey also made a special video about Virgle and the 30 YouTube video contest that is part of the project.

End of Article

The NASA 1975 Preflight PSA briefing included an examination of the instruments on board the Viking craft. A specific instrument was designed to detect the presence of water on Mars. The Viking mission's primary objective was to search for signs of life, which was pursued through various programs such as Photosynthetic Analysis, Metabolic Analysis, Respiration, Molecular Analysis, Inorganic Chemistry, Imaging System, Lander Camera, Entry Science, Water Detection, and more. The Water Detection program is particularly noteworthy, as this was its intended purpose.

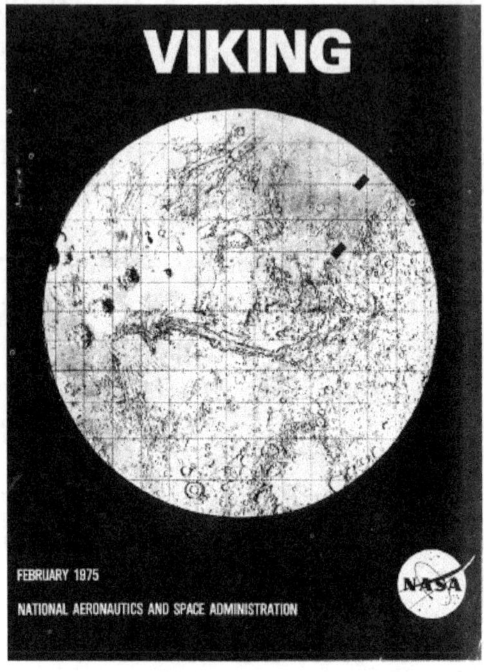

Water Detection (p:13-14)
https://mars.nasa.gov/mro/newsroom/presskits/viking.pdf

The Mars atmospheric water detector on the Viking orbiter can detect very small amounts of water vapor with a high resolution.

The water detector is an infrared spectrometer which operates on the following principle: If water vapor is in the atmosphere, it will absorb a particular part of the infrared light that is produced by the Sun in much the same manner that ozone in our atmosphere absorbs the ultra-violet light, or a yellow filter absorbs all colors except yellow. The infrared spectrometer can determine particular part of the infrared light has been absorbed and how much has been absorbed. This in turn tells the scientists that there is water vapor in the atmosphere and how much.

After the mission was successful NASA released the following PSA brief about the findings of Viking:

NASA Facts

National Aeronautics and

Space Administration

Jet Propulsion Laboratory

California Institute of Technology

Pasadena, CA 91109

NASA Facts

National Aeronautics and
Space Administration

Jet Propulsion Laboratory
California Institute of Technology
Pasadena, CA 91109

Viking Mission to Mars

NASA's Viking Project was the culmination of a series of missions to explore Mars that had begun in 1964 with Mariner 4, and continued with the Mariner 6 and 7 flybys in 1969, and the Mariner 9 orbital mission in 1971 and 1972. Viking found a place in history when it became the first mission to land a spacecraft safely on the surface of another planet.

Two identical spacecraft, each consisting of a lander and an orbiter, were built. Each orbiter-lander pair flew together and entered Mars orbit; the landers then separated and descended to the planet's surface.

Mission Design

Both spacecraft were launched from Cape Canaveral, Florida -- Viking 1 on August 20, 1975, and Viking 2 on September 9, 1975. The landers were sterilized before launch to prevent contamination of Mars with organisms from Earth. The spacecraft spent nearly a year cruising to Mars. Viking 1 reached Mars orbit June 19, 1976; Viking 2 began orbiting Mars August 7, 1976.

After studying orbiter photos, the Viking site certification team considered the original landing site proposed for Viking 1 unsafe. The team examined nearby sites, and Viking 1 landed on Mars July 20, 1976, on the western slope of Chryse Planitia (the Plains of Gold) at 22.3 degrees north latitude, 48.0 degrees longitude.

The site certification team also decided the planned landing site for Viking 2 was unsafe after it examined high-resolution photos. Certification of a new landing site took place in time for a Mars landing September 3, 1976, at Utopia Planitia, at 47.7 degrees north latitude and 48.0 degrees longitude.

The Viking mission was planned to continue for 90 days after landing. Each orbiter and lander operated far beyond its design lifetime. Viking Orbiter 1 exceeded four years of active flight operations in Mars orbit.

The Viking project's primary mission ended

https://atmos.washington.edu/~mars/viking/mission/Viking-don-bane.pdf

The greatest concentration of water vapor in the atmosphere is near the edge of the north polar cap in midsummer. From summer to fall, peak concentration moves toward the equator, with a 30 percent decrease in peak abundance. In southern summer, the planet is dry, probably also an effect of the dust storms.

End of Article.

NASA's 1975 Preflight PSA brief clearly indicates that water was found on Mars and in the atmosphere, yet it is surprising that every subsequent mission seems to discover water for the first time. Virgle, on the other hand, proposed a civilian colonization mission and requested interested individuals to submit their resumes and online videos showcasing how they could contribute to the colony. This April Fool's joke might have fueled the hoax narrative surrounding the Apollo 20 story, given that Space X was founded in 2010 with the exclusive aim of reaching Mars by 2024. Although the 2007 Apollo 20 story may be a hoax, it has links to the 2005 story, which has more realistic and better-quality photos. However, several links to online videos and photos cited in Thierry's book are no longer accessible online, adding to the misdirection surrounding this story.

Apollo 18, 19 and 20 Canceled Missions

Alleged NASA Apollo 18, 19 and 20 patches

Upon further investigation, I delved into the claim that NASA canceled the Apollo 18, 19, and 20 missions in 1970. It is true that these missions were cancelled, but there is controversy surrounding the reasons why. According to my research, all three missions were fully funded, with rockets built and fueled, crews selected and trained, and landing sites and alternative sites already determined. Additionally, the command capsules, LEMs, and rovers had been built. This makes it difficult to believe that NASA canceled these missions solely due to the Apollo 13 disaster and budget constraints, as is NASA's official stance. NASA has also claimed that the Apollo 18 rocket was repurposed for the Skylab missions, which replaced Apollo 18, 19, and 20. The other rockets and craft were put on display at NASA and in the Air and Space Museum, despite the signage for these displays stating they are "replicas" and therefore not the original craft and vehicles.

NASA had selected Copernicus Crater as the landing site for Apollo 18, Hadley Rille (the site Apollo 15 went to) for Apollo 19, and Tycho Crater for Apollo 20. However, JPL, which generally controls NASA launches and programs, had Apollo 18 going to Schröter's Valley, a site that looks like ancient rivers on the moon.

Apollo 19 was to go to Hyginus Rille, a site that looks like ancient volcanic activity on the moon, and then Apollo 20 would go to Copernicus Crater. The center of the Copernicus Crater looks to have derelict dome structures in its center, while the walls of the crater are angled and terraced much like what we would see at strip mining sites on Earth.

Despite the official reason for the cancellation of these missions, it is possible that they were replaced by a fully funded mission set, that of Skylab 1, 2, and 3. Skylab was a unique mission that required all new vehicles for a space orbital platform used for scientific purposes and research. Each mission required multiple launch vehicles to get the labs into space, the crew, and supplies. It is possible that these launches could have covered a secret mission or missions of Apollo 18, 19, and 20 to the back side of the moon, as all attention would have been directed towards the Skylab program.

No Soviet/NASA Missions During the Cold War

The third claim was about joint Soviet/NASA missions during the Cold War. However, it is worth noting that Skylab 2 and 3 were joint Soviet/NASA missions during the same period. This raises the question of what the Cold War was truly about if the US and the USSR were collaborating in space, the ultimate military high ground, despite being sworn enemies.

NASA, (Never A Straight Answer) has a reputation for being evasive, so it may be difficult to determine the truth, but it appears that the three hoax claims have been largely debunked.

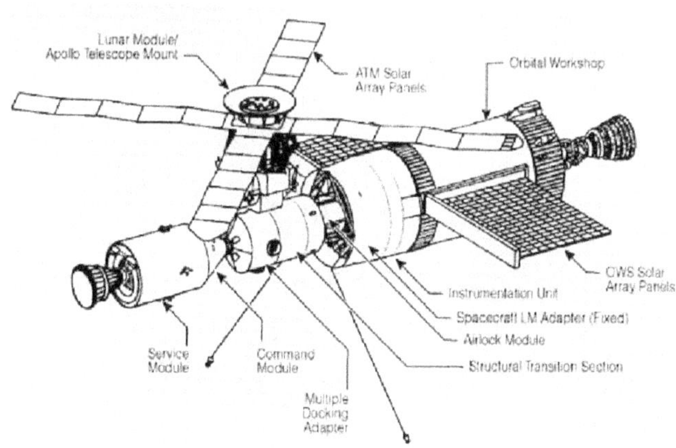

Reuters Apollo 20 Factcheck

On December 15th, 2022, Reuters put out a Fact Checking article about Apollo 20, beating a dead horse hoax narrative again. In their claim, they stated that:

"Human remains have never been found on the moon, NASA's chief historian told Reuters, but users online are sharing a video that is allegedly proof a sarcophagus named Mona Lisa was discovered during a moon mission. The video appears to originate from a fictional story about an Apollo 20 mission, which never happened according to NASA, created by a French author."

Fact Check-No evidence of human remains dubbed 'Mona Lisa' found on the moon.

By Reuters Fact Check: December 15, 2022

https://www.reuters.com/article/factcheck-mona-lisa-moon/fact-check-no-evidence-of-human-remains-dubbed-mona-lisa-found-on-the-moon-idUSL1N3351X5

The fact check article concludes by stating that the three Apollo 20 hoax claims have been debunked, and the provided evidence supports NASA's official stance on the matter. Additionally, the article mentions the 2017 video interview with Thierry Speth, which features a poor reproduction of the Mona Lisa face and does not live up to the original story or photographs. Overall, the fact check article discredits the Apollo 20 hoax and encourages readers to approach similar conspiracy theories with a critical eye.

VERDICT

False. There is no evidence that human remains were found on the moon, a NASA spokesperson told Reuters, and the footage appears to originate from a fictional story about an Apollo 20 mission."

I commend Reuters for their accuracy in fact-checking, but also criticize them for being entirely incorrect. While they correctly state that no human remains or sarcophagus were found on the moon, they missed the mark in other areas. The original story never mentions a sarcophagus, and it never claims that the remains found were human, or dead for that matter. In fact, the beings depicted in the photographs bear a striking resemblance to the Dropa and or Drokpa, an extraterrestrial race believed to originate from Sirius, but nomadic to Tibet and South Asia today. While their fact-checking skills are commendable, Reuters seriously missed the mark in this instance.

It's worth noting that a YouTube channel called the Why Files recently published a video on this hoax narrative in February 2023. However, they simply repeated the poorly researched information without conducting further research into the topic. Drama and clicks seem to dominate real research these days. It's strange that they decided to cover this topic now, 16 years after it was already considered a hoax, why? It's possible that they did it for the sake of generating online traffic or perhaps to divert attention from other disclosures that have been made at the government level. These questions lead back to the Chinese announcement in 2021 that they planned to build a cigar-shaped generation ship in Earth's orbit. Could this be connected to the alleged discovery of the Dropa crashed ship in Bayan Kara Ula after the 1950 invasion of Tibet, or what Yutu-2 discovered while flying over the back side of the moon to its south pole destination? While these are high-octane speculations, the timing of these events is interesting and appears to suggest the existence of a compartmentalized secret space project involving the Chinese and other government or agency actors.

Conclusions of the Dropa Research

In my view, the alleged hoax surrounding the Dropa Stones, and their lore and legends appears to be a deliberate attempt to deceive and mislead anyone investigating this fringe topic. However, my research has revealed that the stories contain many factual and cultural elements that cannot be ignored. Additionally, there are translation and transliteration issues related to the names of people, places, and cultures involved, as well as references to technologies that were not available or invented at the time of the original story or publication. The overwhelming misdirection around the high-octane speculations of secret NASA and space missions further complicates the investigation. Despite this, I believe that there is sufficient evidence to justify further research into the Dropa Stones and their potential cultural and historical significance.

Key Conclusive Takeaways:

1. The Dropa or Drokpa People are a real ethnic group known for their short stature, orange yellow skin, deep blue, and green eyes, and they speak an ancient regional language called Brokkat and Brokskat of Shina dialect, which predates Sanskrit the mother language of the region.

2. The Dropa or Drokpa People are nomadic and traverse from their original home in far east Kham Tibet through Tibet, Bhutan, northern India, Nepal, Ladakh, Pakistan, Kashmir, Afghanistan, Turkmenistan, and eventually reach the Black Sea area. Interestingly, even Hungarian Táltos shamans share similarities in language, rituals, and appearance.

3. In the 1950s, the Chinese invasion of Tibet resulted in the eradication of many Tibetan clans as they advanced towards Lhasa, forcing some into a nomadic lifestyle, much like the Drokpa.

4. The Dropa Stones, initially described during the 1938 expedition, bear resemblance to the mysterious and enigmatic Bi Disks of the region. They might or might not have an extraterrestrial origin; however, they do exhibit piezoelectric anomalies and contain infusions of Cobalt and Mercury, giving them a battery-like storage quality.

5. The original 1964 and 1967 Dropa story publications suffer from translation and transliteration issues, having been translated from Chinese to German, then to Russian, French, and finally English. Consequently, the names Chi Pu Tei and Tsum Un Nui do not have Chinese origins, but could be names misheard.

6. Due to transliteration, it is likely that Chi Pu Tei is Shifu Tei, meaning "master" or "teacher," with Tei being a western transliteration of Teochew, a popular Chinese name. Similarly, the name Tsum Un Nui is likely Tsuong Nguyen, a combination of a Hao Chinese Vietnamese name. Additionally, Dropa is likely transliterated as Dzopa, Drokpa, and Brokpa across the nomadic regions of South Asia.

7. The Ham Chinese mentioned in the text do not exist as a cultural group in Tibet or China. It is more likely that the reference is a transliteration of the Kham Tibetans who do exist and in my opinion, tell the story found on the Dropa stone with writing on it, as found in the 1964 UFO Nachrichten publication.

8. The Beijing Academy of Sciences and Prehistory, known as such before 1949, is now recognized and was re-established as the Chinese Academy of Sciences, located in Beijing, with Prehistory being one of its departments.

9. Dr. Karyl Robin-Evans, claimed to be a fake name and Oxford professor, might be the same person as Dr. Karl Evans of Oxford, a professor of sociology and anthropology during the same time period, making him a real person in my opinion.

10. "Sungods in Exile" incorporates various Tibetan, Bhutanese, and Buddhist cultural aspects that researchers from the 1940s-1970s could not have known, including rituals, religious practices, and even the sexual promiscuity known to the Drokpa, and the people of Bhutan.

11. "Sungods in Exile" also describes technologies such as solid-state hard drives, fiber optics, and flat screen curved consoles, which had not yet been invented during the time the book was published.

12. "Sungods in Exile" also depicts remarkable and seemingly unbelievable feats of Nepalese porters and high-altitude naked meditating monks. However, with the now known altitude component of the DNA of Nepalese Sherpas and the achievements of individuals like the "ice man" Wim Hof, these skepticisms can be put to rest.

13. The author of "Sungods in Exile" claims the book is a hoax in Fortean Times, 1994 and 1998, under the slightly different name of David Gamon. However, the side column stories do not read like a tell-all admission and could have been penned by anyone.

14. Examples of generation ships can be found in science fiction stories, secret NASA space missions, as well as in ancient texts such as the Vedic epic story of the Mahābhārata, a 2200-year-old Buddhist poem called the Lotus Sutra, the the Zen Japanese Utsuro-Bune story, and, in my opinion, with the scientific data derived from the discovery of the interstellar object, Oumuamua.

15. The original stories are said to have appeared in two unknown publications as well as popular Sputnik Magazine,

from 1962, and in Chariots of the Gods from 1968. However, during my research, I couldn't find these articles or stories or these publications. Instead, they seem to be present in a different series of publications from 1964 and 1967. This raises the possibility of a deliberate misdirection by the UFO community, poor research, or a combination of both.

16. There is a strong connection between Sirius and Buddhist mysticism, which could not have been known during the 1940-1970 period. However, this connection does appear in ancient Buddhist poetic verses and stories of Ascended Tulku Masters who have mastered the meditational spiritual technology of astral projection. It also appears in the legends of Mount Meru and the rainbow bridge of dimensional travel from its summit, which is used to transport gifts and Ascended Tulku Masters to and from Sirius.

17. Ancient Buddhist caves have existed throughout China, Nepal, Bhutan, eastern Kham Tibet, and the Bayan Kara Ula and Bayan Har Shan Mountains for at least 16,000 years.

18. Shambala, a dimensional inner earth portal of Mount Meru, is speculated to be the resting place of the four gifts from Sirius. These gifts were the foundational pillars of Buddhism, existing 10,000 years prior to Siddhārtha Gautama, also known as Śākyamuni Buddha. It is worth noting that Śākyamuni Buddha is considered the first Buddha and Bodhisattva, but according to my research, he is only an incarnation of the first Buddha.

19. Pyramids and a peculiar culture known as Sanxingdui have existed in easter Tibet and the central China regions for at least 3,000 years. Unfortunately, much of China's prehistory, including the Sanxingdui culture, remains unknown due to the destructive impact of the 1966 Chinese Maoist Cultural Revolution. This culture also exhibits connections to the Kham of Tibet, the Cham of Cambodia, and even the Olmec of Central America.

Based on my research, I have found compelling information that leads me to directly associate the Dropa people with the Drokpa nomadic group and their origins from Sirius approximately 12,000 years ago. This connection is supported by evidence found in the Mahābhārata and ancient Buddhist manuscripts, mysticism, and practices. In my opinion, these findings provide a strong basis for this correlation.

As this is a soft version of my research, and there are many breakaway topics to be considered, I look forward to sharing more of my research through upcoming lectures and books.

•••

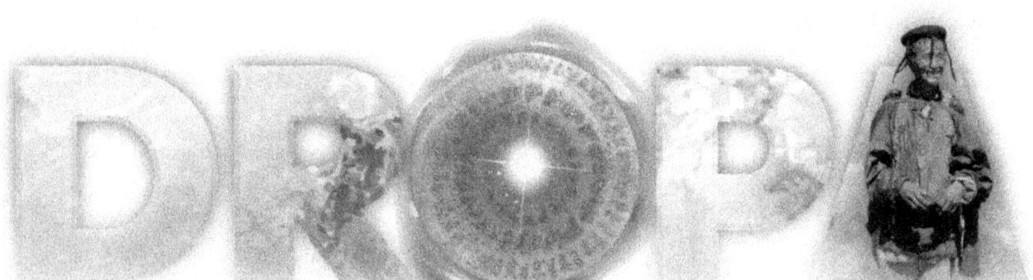

www.ingramcontent.com/pod-product-compliance
Lightning Source LLC
LaVergne TN
LVHW010918110826
845149LV00013B/2415

9798993637815